WHAT A YEAR IT WAS!

1954

A walk back in time to revisit
what life was like in the year that
has special meaning for you...

*Congratulations
and
Best Wishes*

To

From

DEDICATION

To: Peter Hess
As we complete our 20th book together, thank you so much for making the
WHAT A YEAR IT WAS! series a most joyful, creative, fun experience and
for your unending patience and wonderful spirit. Here's to the next 20!

Series Created By • Beverly Cohn
Designers • Peter Hess & Marguerite Jones
Research • Laurie Cohn

Special thanks to Kenny Bookbinder for his invaluable help with the Sports section.

CONTENTS

POLITICS & WORLD EVENTS

U.S. Explodes First H-Bomb

Here on Eniwetok Island, the cab or housing for the first hydrogen bomb takes shape after months of preparation.

I**n this building, the cataclysmic force of the H-bomb will be released.**

W**orking as a task force team, the Army, Navy and Air Force work against time to prepare the installations, under the supervision of scientists who have labored for years to develop the thermonuclear weapon. Eniwetok, the target island, is almost ready for the sacrifice.**

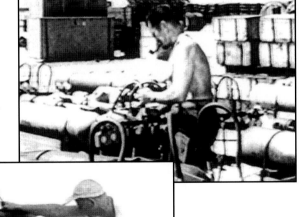

continues on next page

WHAT A YEAR IT WAS!

U.S. Explodes First

The island is connected with two others by a plywood tube. Filled with helium, it houses the hundreds of instruments that will record the explosion data, which is the prime objective of the test.

With final preparations almost complete, jeeps with workers leave the island.

The ball of fire is three miles across as it shatters both land and sea. The shock wave races 35 miles and reaches the control ship with enough force to jar the solidly mounted camera.

Observers are instructed to not remove goggles or face the burst until 10 seconds after the first light.

WHAT A YEAR IT WAS!

H-Bomb cont.

Under the direction of General Clarkson, Task Force Commander (top left)*, the countdown begins.*

Rising with the cloud are millions of cubic feet of radioactive ash, a virulent by-product of the fusion bomb that will shower down over the area in approximately one hour. With its force measured in megatons equivalent to millions of tons of TNT, the power of the thermonuclear bomb is almost inconceivable.

In seconds the fireball erupts into a geyser that towers 25 miles into the stratosphere, spreading into a 100-mile-wide mushroom cloud.

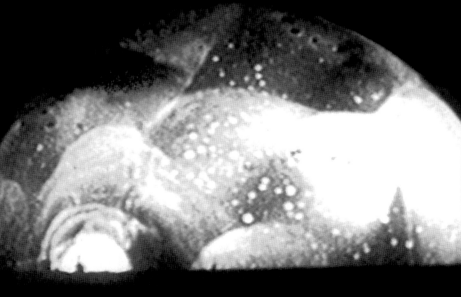

As never before, man holds the seeds of his own destruction. Humanity stands at a grim crossroad in the age of the atom.

1954

U.S.S. NAUTILUS
SSN 571
KEEL LAID JUNE 14, 1952
DECLIVITY ¹¹/₁₆ TO 1 FT.

FIRST ATOMIC-POWERED SUB LAUNCHED

At Groton, Connecticut, a new naval era dawns with the launching of the Nautilus, one of the largest submarines ever built, and the first atomic-powered craft in history. It is believed that the Nautilus will probably initiate a revolution in naval warfare.

About 20,000 people are on hand to witness this momentous occasion.

Mrs. Dwight D. Eisenhower arrives to christen the historic vessel built at a cost of $55 million and capable of cruising around the world without resurfacing because its atomic engine requires no air.

The historic moment is at hand.

The launching cradle is released and as the *Nautilus* slides down the ramp, Mrs. Eisenhower christens it with a valiant blow.

In the yards below, Commander Eugene P. Wilkinson, skipper of the atomic sub, will oversee the actual launching just seconds away.

The *Nautilus* is officially launched and begins its slide into the water.

With its pioneer model atomic power plant, the Nautilus has an underwater speed of over 30 knots, making it capable of outrunning all but the fastest surface vessels while remaining submerged. At once a formidable fighting ship and a forerunner of commercial atomic power, the Nautilus heralds a new era of the atomic age.

WHAT A YEAR IT WAS!

Model 21K12, with 21″ screen, walnut finish, $299.95. UHF optional, at extra cost. Prices include Fed. Ex. Tax and full year warranty on all parts, tubes and picture tube. Slightly higher South and West. Subject to change without notice.

New design eliminates glare and tone-loss!

Glare down tilted screen eliminates reflections for **perfect viewing!**

Sound up design directs sound upward to ear level for **perfect listening!**

Seat yourself before a beautiful big-screen Motorola TV and thrill to a new experience in television: New clarity of vision *at eye level* . . . new richness of tone *at ear level!* It's Motorola's Glare Down/Sound Up cabinet design! The forward-tilted Glare Guard screen deflects unwanted reflections to the floor, to allow you clear, glare-free viewing. The tilted-back Golden Voice speaker directs tone *up* for easy listening. Picture and sound are brought together in thrilling realism! New Fashion Academy Award styling! And remember this: Every Motorola TV set made today will receive color telecasts too, in fine black-and-white, for years of big-screen entertainment.

Better See the Motorola TV Hour on ABC-TV, Tuesday nights in most cities

Better See **Motorola TV**

with **DOUBLE-POWER PICTURE**

"Golden Voice" Reg. U. S. Pat. Off. ©1954, Motorola Inc.

9

1954 BERLIN *Conference*
OF FOREIGN MINISTERS IS STORMY

Britain's Anthony Eden, who staunchly supports the West's demand for German-Austrian peace talks *(left)*, is followed by America's John Foster Dulles, who spearheads the attack on the Soviets' demand for a future parley to include Red China *(right)*.

Andre Gromyko *(exiting car)* accompanies Soviet Foreign Minister Molotov, who has proposed, in effect, the carving up of the world under spheres of big power influence, bypassing the United Nations.

Joining determined resistance to this move is France's Georges Bidault, who refuses to buy peace in Indochina from the Communists.

As the third session opens, Molotov again seeks to delay German peace talks by proposing a disarmament conference, a move vigorously opposed by Mr. Dulles.

A deadlock on an acceptable agenda for the conference becomes tighter, as the Western bloc of statesmen stick firmly to their intentions of discussing matters dealing only with the peace of Europe. So far, it's a stalemate.

WHAT A YEAR IT WAS!

10

GERMANY
East & West

German Chancellor Konrad Adenauer tells 1,000 freed POWs that Germany is purified of Hitlerism.

West Berlin gives sanctuary to 305,000 refugees from East Berlin.

Ending a monthlong truce, East and West Berlin dump thousands of leaflets on each other.

Russians reject the idea of German reunification.

Theodor Heuss is elected president of West Germany.

Four hundred are arrested in East Germany as U.S. spies.

French Assembly accepts West Germany as armed ally.

NATO *nations reach agreement on arming and admitting West Germany.*

EUROPE

FRANCE AND WEST GERMANY SIGN CULTURAL AND ECONOMIC AGREEMENT.

BRITAIN OPENS TRADE TALKS IN LONDON WITH HUNGARY.

Yugoslavia's Marshal Tito rules out Soviet-style centralized government and economy.

Making it clear that he will not tolerate a drift toward Western-style Democracy, Yugoslavia's Marshal Tito removes Milovan Djilas, who is critical of Tito, from the Communist Central Committee.

Marshal Tito

While insisting on peaceful coexistence, Marshal Tito and Jawaharlal Nehru reject plan for neutral third bloc.

VISITING? CALL LONG DISTANCE FIRST

EXPECTED
*guests
are doubly*

When you're going to stop and visit out-of-town friends, it's a good idea to telephone ahead.

You'll enjoy your trip more knowing they'll be home. Your welcome will be all the warmer because you're expected.

Long Distance is the convenient, friendly way to make plans or confirm them. And the cost is small.

LONG DISTANCE RATES ARE LOW Here are some examples:		You
New York to Philadelphia ...	40¢	save time
Cleveland to Louisville	75¢	when you
St. Louis to Houston.........	$1.10	Call by
Miami to Indianapolis.......	$1.35	Number
Boston to Los Angeles.......	$2.00	

These are the Station-to-Station rates for the first three minutes, after 6 o'clock every night and all day Sunday. They do not include the federal excise tax.

Bell Telephone System

Don't wonder. Don't worry.
Call today and be sure.

12

IF SWEET SOFT DRINKS
LEAVE YOU THIRSTY...

SWITCH TO *Squirt*

Never an after-thirst!

Fresh clean taste
<u>as</u> you drink Squirt
...fresh clean taste
<u>after</u> you drink Squirt
...never an
after-thirst!

When you serve mixed drinks,
and when you drink, be
smooth about it... Switch to
Squirt, the SMOOTH mixer.

COPYRIGHT 1954, THE SQUIRT COMPANY
BEVERLY HILLS, CALIF.

United States

U.S. and Canada agree to build radar warning stations across northern Canada to give warning of approaching aircraft or missiles over the Arctic.

U.S. signs pact with Nationalist China.

Governor General Massey is first Canadian leader to address both houses of U.S. Congress.

President Eisenhower and Winston S. Churchill meet in Washington and sign Potomac Charter.

In the biggest midterm voter turnout in the U.S., Democrats regain control of the House and Senate with Sam Rayburn and Lyndon Johnson to head House and Senate.

Lyndon B. Johnson

U.S. Ambassador to Italy **Clare Boothe Luce** is accused of interfering in Italy's internal affairs.

Ike says he can think of no greater tragedy than for the U.S. to get involved in Indochina.

While there is little opposition on Capitol Hill to financially supporting the French operation in Vietnam to the tune of $750 million, President Eisenhower is strongly criticized for sending an Air Force technical mission of 200 men to support the French.

U.S. bars aid in Indochina until French step up military efforts.

President Eisenhower warns that a Communist victory in Indochina will set off a chain reaction in Asia.

President Eisenhower calls Communism a global peril that cannot be checked by armed strength alone.

Eisenhower dispatches Seventh Fleet to protect Taiwan from invasion.

President Eisenhower approves plan for training of South Vietnamese army.

President Eisenhower reports in his State of the Union address that the U.S. has "just completed the most prosperous year in its history" and was capturing "the initiative" in foreign affairs.

President Eisenhower

A TRIBUTE TO 5th NATO's BIRTHDAY

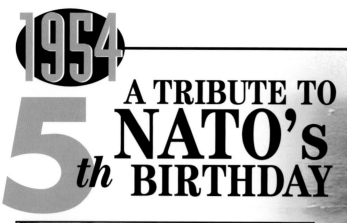

As a tribute to NATO's fifth birthday, Atlantic Treaty naval and air forces are put through rigorous tests in the Mediterranean during one of the most extensive maneuvers of its five-year-old existence.

American, British and French sea and air forces make a close-knit team as they ward off a simulated submarine attack between Gibraltar and Malta.

The main objective of "Exercise Medflex" is to increase the flexibility and coordination of the participating units.

No operation of this magnitude is accomplished without minor casualties and this jet plane hits the ground with crippled landing gear.

It skids to a safe landing and the pilot walks away uninjured. A fighting force takes shape.

WHAT A YEAR IT WAS!

U.S.S.R.

Moscow offers to join NATO if the West will join Soviet-European security treaty.

Soviet Ambassador **Georgy Zarubin** in Washington to discuss international atomic energy pool with Secretary of State **John Foster Dulles**.

John Foster Dulles

While on a reconnaissance flight in Korea, **U.S. downs Soviet MiG.**

Soviet jets down U.S. patrol plane over Sea of Japan.

GEORGY MALENKOV
becomes premier of U.S.S.R.

PURGE

Kremlin purges reach Moldavia, Kazakhstan and Lithuania.

The U.S.S.R. purges 3,000 Georgia party members in two years.

NIKITA S. KHRUSHCHEV

plays major role in Moscow as a result of judicious use of his vast patronage powers in his role as head of the Communist Party.

Nikita Khrushchev

1954—Tetouan
CAPITAL OF Spanish Morocco
CENTER OF ANOTHER TROUBLE SPOT IN NORTH AFRICA

10,000 Arab and Berber tribesmen gather to seek the aid of Spain in ridding themselves of the French-appointed sultan, Sidi bin Arafa, who is their spiritual leader as well as ruler of French Morocco.

Franco's high commissioner, Rafael Garcia Valeño, listens to their pleas.

The official protest is contained in a lengthy document *(above)* that is read to the accompaniment of Arab chants and dances *(right)*.

Tension mounts between France and Spain, as secession looms.

Men Of The
Foreign Legion
Have A Home At Last

Here on their 200-acre farm, men of 52 nations, many of them political exiles from their home countries, enter a new life.

*T*hese men have seen the face of war at the four corners of the globe.

*T*hose who have known the savagery of Indochina receive France's highest decorations before they find peace in their new retreat at the mouth of the Rhône River.

*V*eterans of a corps of desperate men, they have shed their blood for France on desert sands and in steaming jungles.

*L*eisure time is spent playing a friendly game of cards.

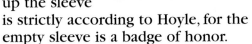

*H*ere an ace up the sleeve is strictly according to Hoyle, for the empty sleeve is a badge of honor.

The shadows of North Africa and Indochina are behind them as they look forward to the years of peace they have so richly won.

1954
The Middle East

Citing plans for a major military base in Greece, Britain denies Cypriot request for union with Greece.

British troops fire into rioting crowds as violence erupts during protest strikes and student demonstrations in Nicosia, Cyprus.

King Saud appoints Prince Faisal prime minister.

EGYPT

Britain and Egypt reach an agreement on a Suez Canal pact ending 72 years of British military occupation.

Egypt's Lieutenant Colonel Gamal Nasser challenges General Mohammed Naguib, who quits as president and premier after the revolutionary council resists giving him absolute autocratic authority.

General Mohammed Naguib wins back posts as premier and head of the ruling military junta.

Lieutenant Colonel Gamal Nasser replaces General Mohammed Naguib as premier for second time in two months.

Following an assassination attempt on Gamal Nasser's life, the Muslim Brotherhood is dissolved.

General Mohammed Naguib is placed under arrest as Gamal Abdel Nasser assumes full power in Egypt.

MOROCCO

Eleven die in Morocco riots as nationalists demonstrate against the sultan appointed by the French.

French Legion troops seize Fez Arab quarter in Morocco following riots.

WHAT A YEAR IT WAS!

MAN-it's Super-Charged!

NEW [TOP OCTANE] Sky Chief

SUPER-CHARGED with **PETROX**

delivers **EXTRA POWER**

. . . **EXTRA GASOLINE MILEAGE!**

PROVED . . . by more than a million miles of testing: New Sky Chief, Super-Charged with PETROX, an exclusive petroleum base element developed by Texaco engineers, assures you . . .

MAXIMUM POWER—yet actually CUTS ENGINE WEAR! Valves, valve guides, valve seats, pistons and piston rings are protected against wear, glazing and harmful deposits. Ring wear on test cars reduced up to 45% . . . *spark plug life and efficiency extended over 300%!*

A CLEANER, SMOOTHER ENGINE. Intake system deposits cut down as much as 38%. Extra engine cleanliness like this means smoother, knock-free power.

TRUE ECONOMY. Your engine stays younger. Maximum power with less wear means lower repair bills — and real extra gasoline mileage you can check.

CLIMATE CONTROL. New top octane Sky Chief is 100% *Climate-Controlled* — specially blended for top performance wherever you drive, in each one of the 25 weather areas of the U.S.A., as established by Texaco engineers.

Get this new smoothness, new responsiveness — quicker starts, warm-ups, get-aways, knock-free power a-plenty on the highways, up the hills. Fill up today at your Texaco Dealer, *the best friend your car has ever had.*

WHAT IS PETROX? Petrox is a new element, or additive, wholly derived from petroleum. Developed by Texaco engineers, Petrox is an exclusive Texaco product.

It is a petro-chemical completely different in composition from any other additive. It is the only such additive being used in any gasoline. The fact that it is made entirely from petroleum is important because it does not contain anything that can leave harmful engine deposits.

Furthermore, Petrox adds a brand new function: the ability to reduce engine wear. As a result, the consistent users of new Sky Chief gasoline are assured maximum power and longer engine life.

TOP OCTANE **Sky Chief**

Super-Charged with PETROX

at **TEXACO DEALERS** in all 48 states

Texaco Products are also distributed in Canada and Latin America

THE TEXAS COMPANY

asia

Mongolia

China

Tibet

Nepal

India

Burma

Laos

Thailand

Cambodia

Ceylon

At the Berlin Big Four Conference, British Foreign Secretary Anthony Eden announces a better understanding among France, Britain, America and the Soviet Union with regard to meeting with Communist China to settle the Korean question and to seek peace in Indochina.

Southeast Asia Treaty Organization (SEATO) is established.

KASHMIR ASSEMBLY ACCEPTS REUNIFICATION WITH INDIA.

PRESIDENT EISENHOWER AND U.N. SECURITY COUNCIL VETO INTERVENTION IN RED CHINA-TAIWAN CONFLICT.

Burma and Japan sign treaty.

British airliner downed off Hainan coast by two Chinese MiGs.

Communist oil tanker is struck by Nationalist Chinese planes off Fukien coast.

U.S. reconnaissance plane downed over Japanese island of Hokkaido by Soviet MiGs.

Communist China sinks Nationalist warship off Tachen Islands.

Peking announces that 13 U.S. fliers shot down in 1952 have been sentenced to four years to life for espionage.

Nationalist Chinese sink eight Communist gunboats in Formosa Strait.

Chinese Premier and Foreign Minister **CHOU EN-LAI** announces intention of attacking Taiwan.

Asian conference in Ceylon ends with plea for peace in Indochina, end of atomic tests and condemnation of colonialism.

MAO TSE-TUNG is reelected to another four-year term as Chairman of the People's Republic of China.

Malayan Communists pushed out to Sumatra by the British.

Offering $100 million in aid within three months, the U.S. signs defense pact with Japan.

The United Nations Command withdraws from last North Korean area, leaving North and South Korea separated by a narrow strip of no-man's land.

FOLLOWING THE ARREST OF 40 PEOPLE INVOLVED IN A NATIONALIST SPY RING IN PEKING, 13 ARE EXECUTED.

U.S. AND TAIWAN SIGN MUTUAL DEFENSE TREATY.

HOLLAND AND INDONESIA DISSOLVE UNION.

WHAT A YEAR IT WAS!

...Vietnam

France and **Vietnam** open talks in Paris on a treaty to form an Indochinese state.

SAIGON ANNOUNCES VIET MINH ASSAULT ON DIEN BIEN PHU.

French forces in Vietnam have their backs against the wall as Communist guerrillas advance and tighten the noose around the airfield at Dien Bien Phu.

U.S. begins flying French paratroopers to Vietnam.

French resistance collapses after a nearly two-month brutal siege of Dien Bien Phu, which falls to the Communists.

Secretary of State John Foster Dulles warns China that the U.S. will retaliate against aggression in Indochina.

French Premier Pierre Mendès-France and Chinese Premier Chou En-lai reach agreement at a meeting in Bern, Switzerland on the basic terms for a political settlement for Indochina.

French troops begin withdrawal from Tonkin.

The U.S., Britain and France reach an agreement in Geneva on Indochina armistice, dividing Vietnam along 18th parallel.

In hiding for eight years, Communist leader Ho Chi Minh returns to Hanoi to assume his rule.

Admitting that it is not a perfect peace, France signs armistice agreements with the Viet Minh in Geneva dividing Vietnam in half along the 17th parallel, with the Communists controlling the north and Emperor Bao Dai controlling the south with French support.

IN SAIGON, head of state Ngo Dinh Diem urges faster withdrawal of French troops.

WHAT A YEAR IT WAS!

THE MAU MAU THREAT

British Colonial Secretary Oliver Littleton *(right)* is greeted at the airport as he arrives in Kenya for a firsthand inspection of the jungle war against the Mau Mau terror organization, whose mandate is to drive the white man out of Africa.

The cabinet minister visits his troops.

He joins a typical jungle patrol, carrying his own rifle and 50-pound pack.

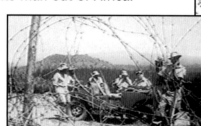

The capture by one of these patrols of General China, a Mau Mau leader, has brought the first contact with the enemy's leadership and the first hope in months of arranging an end to the bloody Mau Mau campaign of terror.

Following the collapse of negotiations for their surrender, over 700 Mau Mau activists are arrested in Kenya by the British.

WHAT A YEAR IT WAS!

LATIN AMERICA

U.S. CONVENES ORGANIZATION OF AMERICAN STATES IN CARACAS TO DISCUSS THE THREAT OF COMMUNISM.

JUAN PERÓN

In his first official act since his reelection, Argentine President Juan Perón arrests four leaders of the opposition party.

Guatemala

A COUP of insurgents and anti-Communist army chiefs forces the end of Guatemalan President Jacobo Arbenz Guzman's pro-Communist regime.

REBELS in Guatemala launch revolt by land, sea and air. New regime arrests 2,000 Communists.

Nicaragua

Following an assassination attempt on President Anastasio Somoza, martial law is imposed in Nicaragua.

Cuba

Batista

Charging that Batista rigged the vote, Ramon Grau San Martin quits Cuban presidential race.

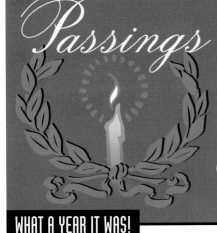

Passings

ROBERT JACKSON, 62

Supreme Court Justice Jackson was appointed to the Court in 1941 by President Roosevelt. In 1945 President Truman named him Chief U.S. Counsel at Nuremberg, where he helped convict 18 Nazi war criminals.

HOYT S. VANDENBERG, 55

General Vandenberg, a graduate of West Point, was a vital presence in Europe and Africa during World War II where he helped plan Allied invasions. He later became both Chief of Staff of the U.S. Air Force and director of the Central Intelligence Agency.

WHAT A YEAR IT WAS!

Even if you're an experienced traveler, you'll be amazed at the luxury, distinction and comforts of the first-class "Super-6" Clipper lounge

FASTEST TO RIO

...no change of plane from New York to B.A. on new, faster "Super-6" Clippers

Only Pan American offers both deluxe and tourist service on the straight-through route to Rio, Montevideo and Buenos Aires ... One-stop service between New York and Rio.

Six days a week big, new "Super-6" Clippers take off from New York and fly through to Buenos Aires. Express Flight 201, flying three times a week, stops only at Caracas, Rio, Montevideo and Buenos Aires! Ask about other deluxe and tourist flights to additional cities shown on map.

In these new Clippers*—the fastest in Pan American's world-wide fleet—you breathe sky-pure air, changed draftlessly every 90 seconds. You have a big, soft, nylon-upholstered seat, and on first-class service oversize luxurious berths are available (at moderate extra cost).

For reservations, call your Travel Agent or Pan American.

IT'S SUMMER NOW— IN SOUTH AMERICA!

Fly away from winter! Doctors say winter vacations give extra health dividends, improve your efficiency all year long. And giant, new "Super-6" Clippers bring these "Sunshine lands" closer than ever! Here are a few typical Latin American cities to visit—your Travel Agent can suggest others!

From New York to	One Way Tourist	One Way First Class
San Juan†	$64	$100
Port of Spain†	148	196
Caracas	156	192
Belem	236	—
Rio	386	460
São Paulo	386	460
Montevideo	448	543
Buenos Aires	456	549

†Plus 15% tax

Ask about direct "Super-6" Clipper flights from MIAMI to all destinations above, plus Havana, Haiti, Dominican Republic, Curaçao.

More people fly to South America by

PAN AMERICAN

WORLD'S MOST EXPERIENCED AIRLINE

PEOPLE 1954

PRESIDENT EISENHOWER AT THE WHITE HOUSE FOR ONE YEAR

At the White House, President Eisenhower unwraps a surprise gift commemorating his first anniversary in office.

It's a foot-high Steuben glass cup engraved to depict his rise from Kansas farm boy to president, symbolizing the highlights of his distinguished career.

Presented by Vice President Nixon and the cabinet, the Eisenhower cup is a fine example of the glass etcher's art.

An impressive gift that earns an impressive beam of delight from the president *(right)* and the First Lady *(left)*.

Former President HARRY S. TRUMAN Celebrates His 70th Birthday

PRESIDENT TRUMAN poses with his wife and daughter as he gets ready to cut his birthday cake.

DEMOCRATIC LEADERS Mrs. Eleanor Roosevelt and William Averell Harriman are among the many present at the New York party.

MARGARET TRUMAN enjoys a light moment with one of the guests.

MRS. TRUMAN focuses her attention on her husband as he gets ready to speak.

THIS FESTIVE OCCASION gives way to seriousness when Mr. Truman takes the rostrum with a major address aimed at President Eisenhower, emphasizing the importance of maintaining the constitutional balance of powers in the government.

"Today the tasks of leadership falling upon the president spring not only from our national problems but from those of the whole world. Today that leadership will determine whether our government will function effectively, and upon its functioning depends the survival of each of us. And today our government cannot function properly unless it functions constitutionally. Our government cannot function properly unless the president is master in his own house and unless the executive departments and agencies of the government, including the armed forces, are responsible to the president."

WHAT A YEAR IT WAS!

GENERAL WILLIAM F. DEAN IS INDUCTED INTO THE PORT OF STOCKTON NAVY

General Dean is summoned to the "Court of Neptune" as it convenes on the steps of the municipal auditorium in order to bestow a citation on the man whose heroism in Korean combat and in Red captivity inspired the nation.

General Dean reads the citation.

A smiling King Neptune presents the general with a cap bearing the insignia of commodore, which carries with it the freedom of the port.

Sincere civic honors in the lighter vein for one of America's great soldiers.

1954 AWARDS

NATIONAL CONFERENCE
OF CHRISTIANS AND JEWS
**GOLD BROTHERHOOD
AWARD**
DOROTHY SHAVER
President, Lord & Taylor

BOYS CLUBS
OF AMERICA
BOY OF THE YEAR
JERRY WHEELER (15)
Houston, Texas

AMERICAN MEDICAL
ASSOCIATION
**FAMILY DOCTOR
OF THE YEAR**
DR. KARL B. PACE (66)
Greenfield, North Carolina
(practicing for 40 years)

**AMERICAN MOTHER
OF THE YEAR**
**Mrs. Love
McDuffle Tolbert** (65)
Columbus, Georgia

TEACHER OF THE YEAR
WILLARD WIDERBERG
7th Grade Teacher
DeKalb (Illinois) Junior High School

BIG BROTHER OF THE YEAR
CHARLES S. MOTT (79)
Flint, Michigan

**OUTSTANDING
HANDICAPPED
MAN OF THE YEAR**
SAM M. CATHEY
Blind Asheville,
North Carolina judge

FREEDOM AWARD
EDWARD R. MURROW
For his unwavering
position against
Senator Joe McCarthy

JOHN FOSTER DULLES

U.S. CHAMBER OF COMMERCE
OUTSTANDING
YOUNG MEN OF 1954

TERRY BRENNAN (26)
Head football coach
at Notre Dame

ROBERT F. KENNEDY (29)
Chief counsel of the
Senate Investigating
Subcommittee

HAM RICHARDSON (21)
Diabetic amateur
tennis player and
Rhodes scholar

FRANK ROSE (34)
President of
Transylvania College

MAJOR CHARLES YEAGER (31)
Record-setting Air Force jet pilot

WHAT A YEAR IT WAS!

West Point graduate and heavily decorated veteran of 60 combat missions during World War II, **Benjamin Oliver Davis Jr.** becomes the first black general in the Air Force.

Henry Cabot Lodge is reappointed to head the U.S. delegation to the U.N.

Assistant Secretary of Labor **James Wilkins** is first black to attend a Cabinet meeting.

GOD BLESSED IRVING BERLIN

President Eisenhower signs a bill authorizing a gold medal for Irving Berlin for composing so many wonderful popular songs including "God Bless America."

Keep The Music Going

Following being honored by the University of Massachusetts with doctorates for their development of the musical play, Richard Rodgers and Oscar Hammerstein II endow Manhattan's Julliard School of Music with a scholarship to be awarded every year to a promising young singer.

THE UNVEILING OF THE VEIL

Widow of the first prime minister of Pakistan, **Begum Liaquat Ali Khan** is appointed ambassador to the Netherlands, the first Muslim woman to ever hold such a position.

*After winning $800 for correctly naming six out of seven melodies on a television quiz show, **Louis "Satchmo" Armstrong** sends his winnings to New Orleans' Milne Municipal Home for Boys where Satchmo was sent when he was 13 for firing a pistol at the moon on New Year's Eve.*

NELSON ROCKEFELLER

named special foreign policy aide by President Eisenhower.

The Harvard Divinity School receives $1 million from John D. Rockefeller Jr.

HIGH FLYERS

The 1954 Harmon International Aviation Awards are presented to 31-year-old Major Charles E. Yeager, first pilot to break the sound barrier, and 48-year-old Jacqueline Cochran, first woman to fly faster than sound.

AND NOW FOR A CLOSER LOOK AT THAT BLACK HOLE

Albert Einstein receives a special gift of an 8-inch Newtonian F-8 telescope that will be sent to the Elsa and Albert Einstein School in Ben Shemen, Israel.

When Einstein Speaks, Does Washington Listen?

Dr. Albert Einstein turns 75 and in an address to the Emergency Civil Liberties Commission urges intellectuals *"to refuse to cooperate in any undertaking that violates the constitutional rights of the individual."*

WHAT A YEAR IT WAS!

1954 Queen Elizabeth Tours Australia

Now in the fifth week of their tour of the Down Under continent, Queen Elizabeth and Prince Philip are welcomed with incredible enthusiasm.

The royal couple visits Melbourne and, as everywhere else, the town goes wild.

The legendary Aussie enthusiasm surpasses itself.

Hailed as a historic occasion, it's the first time a reigning British sovereign has visited Australia, and the public acclaim of the queen is unparalleled in the nation's history.

This jubilant tribute will be long remembered by both Australia and the royal couple.

WHAT A YEAR IT WAS!

ROYAL GOINGS-ON

Prince Charles, heir apparent to the British throne, celebrates his sixth birthday with a party and tea.

20-year-old Crown Prince Akihito of Japan passes his road test and gains his driver's license.

What's a SEVEN-LETTER WORD Meaning

Extremely Privileged?

Britain's Princess Margaret wins first place in a crossword puzzle contest sponsored by a British magazine.

The Duke of Windsor, former King Edward VII of England, turns 60 and celebrates by sunning himself in the garden of his Paris summer residence.

U.S. crooner Eddie Fisher sends Princess Margaret a special recording of "Happy Birthday to You" in honor of her 24th birthday.

A ROYAL TAKES A SWING

The Duke of Windsor is in Cuba for the four-ball amateur invitation tournament at the Havana Biltmore Yacht and Country Club.

Queen Mother Elizabeth of Britain arrives in New York on the QUEEN ELIZABETH for a 23-day trip to the U.S. and Canada.

Queen Elizabeth II awards 79-year-old
Sir Winston Churchill
the Knight of the Garter, the oldest European chivalric order.

A Day In The Life Of A Queen – Dancing Followed By Shopping

Following dancing at a ball observing the centenary of the Crimean War battle of Balaklava, Queen Elizabeth II goes Christmas shopping for her children, purchasing a three-foot rag doll and doll carriage for four-year-old Princess Anne and a toy death-ray gun and a spaceman game for six-year-old Prince Charles.

Britain's **B**royalty **B**royally entertains Sweden's King Gustav VI and Queen Louise, the first Swedish monarchs to visit Great Britain since 1908.

1954 CONTEST WINNERS

QUEENS KINGS & MISSES

MISS EUROPE
DANIELLE GENAULT (21)*
France

*Original winner Christel Schaak of Germany is disqualified after it was discovered that she is a widow.

BERT PARKS becomes host of the Miss America Pageant.

MISS UNIVERSE
MIRIAM STEVENSON (21)
U.S.A.

MISS WORLD
ANTIGONE COSTANDA
Egypt

MRS. AMERICA
MRS. WANDA JENNINGS (28)
St. Louis, Missouri

ROSE QUEEN
BARBARA SCHMIDT (18)
Pasadena City College

MAID OF COTTON
BEVERLY LOUISE PACK (20)
El Paso, Texas

HAY & GRAIN SHOW CORN KING
WILLARD C. KIRK*
Jeffersonville, Ohio

*Original winners Arnold and Paul Karsk are disqualified for gluing kernels to their sample ears of corn.

MISS INDIAN AMERICA
MARY LOUISE DEFENDER (23)
A Sioux of Fort Yates, North Dakota

WHAT A YEAR IT WAS!

Be nice to your husband

*Present him with these
wonderful grooming aids featured at*

STANLEY HOSTESS PARTIES

SHAVING CREAM

AFTER SHAVE LOTION

LIQUID DEODORANT

COLOGNE

AFTER SHAVE TALC

ADMIRAL HAIR BRUSH

COMMANDER HAIR BRUSH

POCKET COMB & CASE

"LIFETIME" CLOTHES BRUSH

Chairman Line Products come both in bottles (except Shaving Cream) and in the Stanley-Flex containers (fine for traveling) shown above.

Here's a sure way to delight your husband . . . or any man you wish to please. For his birthday, for Christmas, or for anytime you wish to make him particularly happy, remember him with gifts of Stanley's excellent, new "he man" Chairman Line Products and other Stanley Quality Plus Products designed for men. You shop for these, as well as

for many other superior Stanley grooming aids for yourself and children, at Stanley Hostess Parties. At these Parties too, your friendly Stanley Dealer demonstrates Stanley's wealth of Products to save you lots of time and work in practically every housekeeping task. Why not attend, or give, one of these fun-filled Stanley Parties soon?

STANLEY LEADS with more than 150 Quality Plus Products featured exclusively by Stanley Dealers at Stanley Hostess Parties: Toilette Articles, Bath Accessories, Personal and Clothing Brushes, newest scientific aids to Dental Hygiene, many other Personal Grooming items. Mops, Brushes, Dusters, Brooms, Waxes, Polishes, Cleaning Chemicals, Deodorizers, Moth Preventives, other modern "helps" to save you time, work, money, in the better care of your home.

STANHOME
A STANLEY HOME PRODUCT

Originators of the
Famous Stanley Hostess
Party Plan

Stanley Home Products, Inc., Westfield, Mass.
Stanley Home Products of Canada, Ltd., London, Ont.

Millions of homemakers now shop yearly at Stanley's famous Hostess Parties. More than 12,000 of these enjoyable shopping Parties now take place each day. To arrange for your own Stanley Hostess Party, phone or write your Stanley Dealer, your nearest Stanley Home Products Branch Office, or communicate direct with Stanley's main office in Westfield, Mass. *(Copr. Stanley Home Products, Inc., 1954)*

33

1954—Joe & Marilyn

Honeymoon In Japan

Joe DiMaggio and his beautiful bride, Hollywood glamour queen Marilyn Monroe, arrive at Tokyo airport but decide to go back into the plane while police clear a path to the cargo hatch where their convertible awaits them.

A FAN tries to get a closer look at the famous couple.

POLICE TRY to hold back a throng of 4,000 baseball and movie fans who soon surge out of control and break through police lines.

THE STRATEGY works. The former Yankee slugger and his picture bride escape into the car and head for the safety of their hotel.

BUT THE TURMOIL isn't over as the next day comes a press conference.

The public is barred, but the photographers and reporters more than make up for that as their questions are rough, ranging from the risqué to the ridiculous.

MARILYN handles herself with charm and ease.

The photographers are so caught up with Marilyn that for the moment Joe is the forgotten man, which is something in Japan where baseball is so popular.

JOE IS READY to leave and calls an end to the press conference.

JOE ESCORTS MARILYN out of the pressroom.

HEADLINER

Hollywood glamour queen Marilyn Monroe and Yankee Clipper Joe DiMaggio wed in San Francisco's City Hall.

WHAT A YEAR IT WAS!

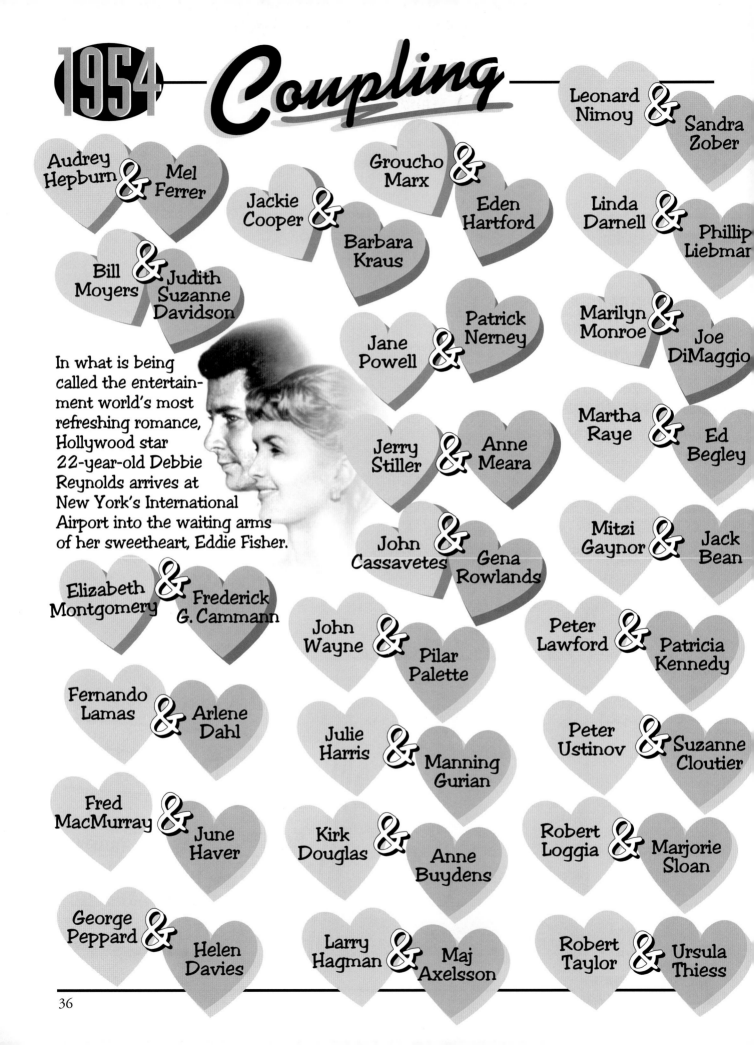

Leonard Nimoy **&** Sandra Zober

Audrey Hepburn **&** Mel Ferrer

Groucho Marx **&** Eden Hartford

Jackie Cooper **&** Barbara Kraus

Linda Darnell **&** Phillip Liebman

Bill Moyers **&** Judith Suzanne Davidson

Jane Powell **&** Patrick Nerney

Marilyn Monroe **&** Joe DiMaggio

In what is being called the entertainment world's most refreshing romance, Hollywood star 22-year-old Debbie Reynolds arrives at New York's International Airport into the waiting arms of her sweetheart, Eddie Fisher.

Jerry Stiller **&** Anne Meara

Martha Raye **&** Ed Begley

John Cassavetes **&** Gena Rowlands

Mitzi Gaynor **&** Jack Bean

Elizabeth Montgomery **&** Frederick G. Cammann

John Wayne **&** Pilar Palette

Peter Lawford **&** Patricia Kennedy

Fernando Lamas **&** Arlene Dahl

Julie Harris **&** Manning Gurian

Peter Ustinov **&** Suzanne Cloutier

Fred MacMurray **&** June Haver

Kirk Douglas **&** Anne Buydens

Robert Loggia **&** Marjorie Sloan

George Peppard **&** Helen Davies

Larry Hagman **&** Maj Axelsson

Robert Taylor **&** Ursula Thiess

Uncoupling 1954

Sally Rand **&** Fred Lalla

Shirley MacLaine **&** Steve Parker

Sonny Bono **&** Donna Rankin

Stanley Kubrick **&** Ruth Sobotka

Steve Allen **&** Jayne Meadows

Vera-Ellen **&** Victor Rothschild

Vic Damone **&** Pier Angeli

Vincente Minnelli **&** Georgette Magnani

W.C. Handy **&** Irma Louise Logan

Jackie Gleason and wife Genevieve legally separate, with Genevieve and their two daughters receiving 14 1/2% of the comedian's estimated $40,000 monthly earnings.

Billy Rose **&** Eleanor Holm

Donald O'Connor **&** Gwen Carter

Fidel Castro **&** Mirta Diaz-Balart

Gloria DeHaven **&** Martin Kimmell

Jane Wyman **&** Fred Karger

Jeff Chandler **&** Marjorie Hoshelle Chandler

Johnnie Ray **&** Marilyn Morrison

Leslie Caron **&** George Hormel

Marie McDonald **&** Harry Karl

Citing conflicting career demands, after less than a year of marriage, Marilyn Monroe sues Joe DiMaggio for divorce.

Susan Hayward **&** Jess Barker

Vittorio Gassman **&** Shelley Winters

Zeppo Marx **&** Marion Benda Marx

DON'T RETURN THE DIAMONDS, DAHLING
Zsa Zsa Gabor is granted a divorce in Santa Monica, California from husband George Sanders on the grounds that he was not cut out for marriage.

1954

TV and radio star **ARTHUR GODFREY** gets his pilot's license revoked for six months for careless flying over the Teterboro, New Jersey airport.

Winner of the Pulitzer Prize four times, 80-year-old poet **ROBERT FROST** takes his first airplane flight to attend an international writers' congress in São Paulo, Brazil.

Martin Luther King, Jr. becomes pastor of the Dexter Avenue Baptist Church in Montgomery, Alabama.

Colin Powell graduates from Morris High School in New York's South Bronx.

John Updike graduates Harvard College.

BARELY ENOUGH TO MAKE ENDS MEET

Winthrop Rockefeller announces that his wife of 6 ½ years, Barbara (Bobo), has agreed to accept a $5,500,000 divorce settlement for her and her son, Winthrop Paul, plus a $500,000 trust fund for the boy.

30-year-old **Marlon Brando** admits to being engaged to 20-year-old Josanne Marianna-Berenger, daughter of a local fisherman in Bandol, France.

TRICKY DICK COULD NOT DO THE TRICK

The U.S. Navy reveals that dereliction of duty was the reason Lt. Commander Richard M. Nixon was denied promotions.

der Bingle

Bing Crosby

BING CROSBY *celebrates his 50th year in Hollywood and says he would like to try non-singing roles.*

involved in a three-car collision in Los Angeles, Bing settles the lawsuit for $100,000.

RITA'S TRIALS & TRIBULATIONS

IN A DIVORCE SETTLEMENT with Prince Aly Khan, Hollywood star Rita Hayworth receives custody of their 5-year-old daughter, Yasmin, and $8,000 a year for support plus $1,000 a month in alimony.

Stemming from his World War II draft exemption as a neutral alien, Rita Hayworth's debt-ridden husband, Dick Haymes, receives deportation orders to his native Argentina on charges of illegally reentering the U.S. after visiting Rita in Hawaii.

Rita Hayworth

The Westchester County Society for the Prevention of Cruelty to Children moves to take Rita Hayworth's two daughters, Rebecca Welles, 9, and Yasmin Khan, 4, away from her on the grounds that they are being neglected and mistreated. The judge orders the children returned to her, saying there is no evidence of willful neglect.

LUCY STAYS AT HOME

Citing that she wants to stay home and take care of her children, the queen of television, Lucille Ball, announces her retirement from the popular *I Love Lucy* show when her contract expires in 1956.

South Of The Border

Hollywood star **GENE TIERNEY** is spending much of her time traveling back and forth to Rosarito Beach, Mexico to meet with her lover, Prince Aly Khan.

Ava Gardner is mobbed by fans in South America while on tour to publicize her latest movie, *The Barefoot Contessa*.

WHAT A YEAR IT WAS!

Stork
REPORT

And Yet Another Great Profile

22-year-old John Barrymore Jr. and the former Cara Williams have their first child, John Barrymore III.

And On A Happy Note

Tony and Patricia Bennett produce their first child, a son named D'Andrea.

ETHEL BARRYMORE, grand dame of the American theater, turns 75.

Happy Birthday, Nicky

Secretary Nikita S. Khrushchev, Russia's No. 3 Communist, turns 58 and receives honors from Premier Georgy Malenkov.

Mrs. Franklin D. Roosevelt turns 70.

Gloria Swanson, 56, reveals that she keeps trim by eating natural foods and doing yoga.

British novelist W. Somerset Maugham celebrates his 80th birthday in London.

WHAT'S BLUE AND YELLOW AND LIVES WITH THE PRESIDENT?

The White House has a new resident—a blue parakeet called Gabby who will live in the cage adjoining High Glory, an orange canary.

"39-year-old" Jack Benny celebrates his 60th birthday.

Famous BIRTHS

- ✓ **Christie Brinkley**
- ✓ **Patty Hearst**

Slicky Handled

Candelabra pianist 34-year-old **LIBERACE** denies rumors that he plans to marry nightclub dancer Joanne Rio but announces that an Oklahoma oil well owned jointly by him and his brother George is flowing at 100 barrels an hour.

This Rich Girl Is No Ugly Duckling

30-year-old millionairess Gloria Vanderbilt Stokowski receives good reviews for her performance in *The Swan* at Pennsylvania's Pocono Playhouse.

Former president Harry S. Truman gets a Social Security card at age 69.

LOCKING HORNS WITH A BEAST

Replete with cape and sword, movie director **JOHN HUSTON** does battle with a small bull with blunted horns in Madrid but is pulled away by his press agent before it becomes a goring experience.

Thanks to the voters in Madison, Wisconsin, crusty 85-year-old architect **FRANK LLOYD WRIGHT** will be hired to design a municipal auditorium and civic center.

WHAT A YEAR IT WAS!

It's A Crime

Virginia Hill

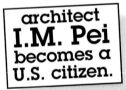

Frank Costello

The Hills Are Alive With Miss Hill

Virginia Hill, girlfriend of the late Bugsy Siegel, is indicted on income tax evasion to the tune of $80,180.02, covering 1944-1947, but is living safely in Austria with her fourth husband, ski instructor Hans Hauser.

Gambler **FRANK COSTELLO** is sentenced to a five-year prison term and $30,000 fine for evasion of $51,095 in income taxes for 1947-1949.

IN SEARCH OF THE ONE-ARMED BANDIT

30-year-old osteopathic surgeon Dr. Samuel H. Sheppard is indicted by a Cleveland grand jury on charges of murdering his wife and is subsequently found guilty of 2nd degree murder.

DOES THE NAME "ITALY" SOUND FAMILIAR?

Racketeer Joe Adonis is given a two- to three-year prison sentence in Hackensack, New Jersey and a $1,000 fine for lying to a county grand jury about his birthplace, which he claims is America.

Maybe You And Joe Can Do Lunch

Deported from the U.S. to Italy, Charles (Lucky) Luciano is placed under two-year parole in Naples on the grounds that the government finds him to be socially dangerous.

---

architect I.M. Pei becomes a U.S. citizen.

PASSPORT NO? *JAIL OUI*

French officials threaten to throw comedian Bob Hope, arriving in Paris to do a television film with Maurice Chevalier, in jail if he doesn't produce his passport in a few hours.

THANK GOD FOR LITTLE CHANGES

After being denied a U.S. visa since 1948 for signing the Stockholm peace petition, Maurice Chevalier is granted a visa to visit America.

Oona O'Neill Chaplin, 28-year-old daughter of the late playwright Eugene O'Neill, renounces her American citizenship and becomes a British citizen.

Aristotle Onassis pays $7 million in fines to the U.S. government after pleading guilty to violating the citizenship provision of U.S. shipping laws requiring that all ships displaying the American flag be owned by citizens.

"THE CRUCIBLE" REVISITED

Playwright **ARTHUR MILLER** is refused a passport because his plays are believed to have supported the Communist movement.

It No Longer Is Because It Isn't

French existentialist-turned-Communist **JEAN-PAUL SARTRE** fails in his attempt to stop the performance at Vienna's Volkstheater of *Dirty Hands*, an anti-Communist play written before he turned Red.

Released from prison after serving 44 months of a five-year perjury sentence, **ALGER HISS** *(right)* maintains that he is innocent of charges brought by Whittaker Chambers that Hiss gave government secrets to a Communist spy ring.

WHAT A YEAR IT WAS!

Ills of the RICH & FAMOUS 1954

Nightclub and television star **Sammy Davis Jr.** suffers loss of his left eye in a car accident near San Bernardino, California.

ERNEST HEMINGWAY
is severely injured in two plane crashes in Nairobi, Kenya.

Democratic Junior Senator from Massachusetts **John F. Kennedy** is recovering from spinal surgery for an injury sustained during World War II when his PT boat was cut in half by a Japanese destroyer.

Former President **Harry S. Truman** is recovering after being rushed to the hospital where emergency surgery is performed to remove his appendix and gall bladder.

Despite suffering from a painful kidney ailment in Düsseldorf, Germany, **Billy Graham** keeps his appearance in Berlin and addresses 75,000 people at the Olympic Stadium.

TV comic **Jackie Gleason** is recovering from a broken right leg and ankle sustained from a fall on his television show.

Jackie Gleason

Faced with an appendectomy, **Ethel Merman** is ordered to bed and put on a diet of baby food with the hopes she can finish her role in the new Irving Berlin musical ***There's No Business Like Show Business***.

Ava Gardner settles down for six weeks in Nevada while awaiting a divorce from her husband, Frank Sinatra.

Ava Gardner

THE WORLD IS HER PLAYGROUND
On advice from her doctors, 25-year-old Hollywood star **Audrey Hepburn** decides to take off for eight months and relax in Switzerland, Italy, France and England.

SAFER IN THE TRENCHES?
Boston Red Sox's **Ted Williams** returns from the Korean War and breaks his collarbone in his first workout with the club.

Almost Didn't Make It Home
Baseball's famed Georgia Peach, **Ty Cobb**, is booked for drunken driving and having no license and is freed on $315 bail.

SLUGGING THIS ONE OUT
Joe DiMaggio checks into a San Francisco hospital for treatment of a duodenal ulcer.

MAKES IT HARD TO PUCKER HIS LIPS AND BLOW
Humphrey Bogart is hospitalized with face cuts after a movie spotlight explodes on the set of *The Desperate Hours*.

LUCKY THING IT WAS ONLY ONE OLIVE
Singer **Johnnie Ray** undergoes surgery for the removal of an abscess on his right foot as a result of stepping on a toothpick that fell out of a martini.

We've Heard Of Playing By Ear, But This Is Ridiculous
While rehearsing with Liberace, **Jimmy Durante** tries playing the piano with his nose only to have the piano lid come down on his famous schnozola.

Jimmy Durante

Passing

Emilie Dionne, 20
One of the famed Canadian Dionne quintuplets, she suffocated in her sleep after several epileptic seizures.

NOT EVEN A CHANGE OF UNDERWEAR?
Marlon Brando's psychiatrist issues a bulletin saying that Brando is "a very sick and mentally confused boy" after he walks off the set of THE EGYPTIAN and flies to New York with only a toothbrush.

Jazz saxophonist **STAN GETZ** receives a 180-day jail sentence for drug addiction.

WHAT A YEAR IT WAS!

41

Look! The glamorous new Cycla-matic Frigidaire with complete Self-Service!

It's the easiest to use food freezer-refrigerator ever made!

NOW I KEEP A WIDE VARIETY OF FOODS ON HAND IN THE HUGE SEPARATE FOOD FREEZER MEAL PLANNING'S EASIER WITH LESS SHOPPING!

THIS REFRIGERATOR DEFROSTS BY ITSELF—NOTHING FOR ME TO DO, EVER! AND LOOK—ALL SHELVES ROLL OUT!

MY NEW PANTRY-DOOR KEEPS BUTTER, CHEESE, EGGS—EVEN LEFTOVERS, HANDY. GIVES ME THIS SERVER TRAY, TOO!

Cycla-matic Imperial Model CTI-103

Ask your Frigidaire Dealer about all the Frigidaire appliances Arthur Godfrey recommends. Look for name in phone book under "Electrical Appliances." Or write Frigidaire, Dept. 2212, Dayton 1, O. In Canada, Toronto, 13 Ont.

If you've been waiting for something really new to happen to refrigerators before you buy—here it is! The Cycla-matic Frigidaire's new concept of *complete* Self-Service makes food-keeping more convenient than ever before. You never have to reach—all food's up front *instantly*. Roll-to-You Shelves glide out all the way with just finger tip pressure. No more groping or playing hide-and-seek with foods.

You can shop way ahead. The completely separate food freezer will keep more than a week's supply of frozen foods safe at zero zone temperatures…has 3 Quickube Ice Trays and 3 Frozen Juice Can Holders.

You never defrost the refrigerator. The Cycla-matic way gets rid of frost *before* it collects. Choose from more Cycla-matic models than ever before—with right or left hand doors at no extra cost!

NEW COLORAMA STYLING glorifies your kitchen! Beautifully styled exteriors are available in two colors or white to match the new Colorama-styled Frigidaire Electric Ranges. Matching porcelain interiors have golden-finished aluminum shelves and trim. Porcelain exterior finish available on many models.

Be modern … live electrically!

Cycla-matic Frigidaire

Built _and_ backed by General Motors

It's Mardi Gras Time In New Orleans

The colorful Proteus Parade moves down St. Charles and the famed Canal Street amid throngs of happy celebrants.

Year after year the Crescent City carnival floats become more and more elaborate *(left) and* the participants make merry in their own mad way.

It's New Orleans' annual whirlwind of gaiety.

Babies Are Still Booming

According to the U.S. Census Bureau, the nation's population continues to increase at the rate of one person every 12 seconds, reaching a new peak of 161,969,000 by May 1st.

Margaret Sanger, the first American woman to address the Japanese Diet, urges use of birth control.

Stork Watch

It appears that Los Angeles edges out Philadelphia by 7,166 people, taking the nation's third-largest-city spot.

TALLER and WIDER

The average American man is growing taller with each generation, having grown .6 inches between World War I and World War II and having added nine pounds to his frame.

YEARLY PER CAPITA ALCOHOL CONSUMPTION
(BURP)

FRANCE:	33 Quarts
ITALY:	15 Quarts
U.S.:	10 Quarts

Vintage White

To try to counter the increasing number of alcoholics, the French government orders schoolchildren to try milk instead of wine.

NEW PUBLICATION

With 350,000 charter subscribers and distribution to newsstands all over the U.S., Time Inc. launches SPORTS ILLUSTRATED.

Repeat After Me: You're Not Really Broke, You're Not Really Broke, You're Not Really B•R•O•K•E
In order to prevent psychological depression, a special Advertising Council committee recommends that space be donated in advertisements to be used for emphasizing favorable factors in the economy.

Coming Soon ...Family Size

For 50 years Coca-Cola has been sold in 6-ounce bottles, but the company announces it will be testing 8- to 12-ounce sizes to meet increasing competition from other soft-drink manufacturers.

Don't Be A Drip – Save A Drop

Mayor Robert F. Wagner orders water conservation measures in New York City.

AMERICAN LIFE EXPECTANCY:

MALE	FEMALE
65.9	**71.8**

AVERAGE: **68.8**

(An increase of almost four years in the last decade)

INDIAN LIFE EXPECTANCY:

(Not Exactly A Ripe Old Age)

MALE	FEMALE
32.45	**31.66**

Metropolitan Life is installing UNIVAC, Remington Rand's big $1,000,000 electronic brain, at its Manhattan home office for use in assembling and analyzing basic actuarial statistics previously handled by clerks.

So Maybe You'll Be A Doctor Or A Dentist?

A seven-year survey conducted under the auspices of the American Bar Association reveals that lawyers may be the most unpopular people in the country and can be traced back to Benjamin Franklin's *Poor Richard's Almanac* in which he wrote: ***"A good lawyer, a bad neighbor."***

You Could Just Die Over This Good News

The Metropolitan Life Insurance Company reports that the U.S. national death rate has dropped to an all-time record low per capita rate of 9.2 deaths per 1,000.

65 And Holding — Oldies But Goodies

Metropolitan Life Insurance publishes a report indicating that a relatively large proportion of American men past the age of 65 are still going to work every day.

Number Of Pets Owned By Americans

(The boids are catching up!)

DOGS	CATS	PARAKEETS
19,600,000	14,600,000	5,000,000

Well, Ain't This The Cat's Meow

Reacting to the worst mad-dog scare in 20 years, Chicago health authorities order all of the city's 350,000 dogs and 250,000 cats vaccinated.

With only 6% of the world population, the U.S. stacks up as follows:

60% of all cars
58% of all telephones
45% of all radios
34% of all railroads

TWO PAPERS BEATING AS ONE

In Los Angeles, Times Mirror buys the <u>Daily News</u> and discontinues its separate publication.

1,768 U.S. newspapers publish 98 million copies daily.

The <u>Washington Times-Herald</u> is sold to the <u>Washington Post</u> and publishes as the <u>Washington Post & Times-Herald</u>.

BASEBALL BLUES

Baseball manufacturing hits a serious slump due to the 40% drop in the number of minor leagues since 1949.

Television Hasn't Taken Its Toll...Yet

The Brooklyn Public Library's annual report shows that circulation has topped eight million books for the first time since the Depression.

It is estimated that more than 85% of all white bread sold in the U.S. is enriched.

Britain ends meat rationing, the last of wartime food controls.

THAT'S A WHOLE LOT OF STEAK

Chicago Union Stockyards receives its *billionth* animal—a Hereford steer.

It's All In A Day's Scrawling

When 850 secretaries are asked if they can read their bosses' handwriting, 41% reply that the penmanship fell somewhere between hard to read to impossible.

The **Fordor Sedan** is one of 5 distinctive *Customline* body styles. Like all Fords, it is powered by a truly modern, deep-block, low-friction engine—either the 130-h.p. Y-block V-8 or the go-packed, thrifty Six.

You can pay more but you can't buy better

You could easily put hundreds of dollars more into your next car and not have all the advances you get in Ford *today*. *All* Fords, for example, are available with the most modern V-8 in the industry, the new 130-h.p. Y-block V-8 . . . *all* Fords bring you new Ball-Joint Front Suspension . . . *all* Fords have clean, graceful lines which will still be in style years from now. So, naturally, when it's time to trade, Fords can be expected to return more per dollar invested than any other car!

The Ford Skyliner—with its picture-window roof—is an "exclusive" in Ford's field. And it's but one of 5 distinguished body styles in the *Crestline* series—each a recognized leader in looks wherever fine cars gather. You couldn't buy better styling at *twice* the price.

The Ford Tudor is one of 4 popular body styles in the lowest priced *Mainline* series. And, like all Fords, it's setting a new standard in riding comfort and handling ease with the greatest advance in chassis design in 20 years—new Ball-Joint Suspension.

Worth More when you buy it
Worth More when you sell it!

it's love at first sight
when schoolkids in Jackson Heights, New York, get a glimpse of the latest in yo-yos and yo-yo techniques.

demonstrators
are mobbed by avid youngsters of all ages, eager to learn all the strings of the spinning sport that's sweeping the country this spring.

just stringing along in the spring

Willie Hoppe's yo-yo hits the side pocket and a good time is had by all.

DOLLARS FOR DEGREES

The Fund for Advancement of Education receives record grant of $25 million from the Ford Foundation.

LET'S SEE, WHAT'S A 7-LETTER WORD ENDING IN "X"?

Help is on the way for Scrabble fans and crossword puzzle nuts searching for words ending in "X," "Y" or "Z" as the University of Massachusetts has just published a reverse dictionary that lists many words by the last letter instead of the first.

ENGINEERS DO IT BETTER AND LONGER!

With one out of every four marriages ending in divorce, the Illinois Institute of Technology releases the good news that no divorces were reported by three of the five classes beginning with 1929.

PUT THOSE BUNSEN BURNERS IN STORAGE

The nation is facing a serious shortage of science teachers.

REALLY HEAVY

What are students at Oklahoma A & M University worried about? You guessed it! Finding parking spaces for their cars.

The first computer put into operation on a commercial basis is rented to Princeton University by Electronic Associates.

But Sir, It's 10 Below And I'm Freezing

Harvard University authorities issue an order that fans may not bring alcoholic beverages to any football games.

245,000 KOREAN WAR VETERANS ARE ENROLLED IN U.S. COLLEGES.

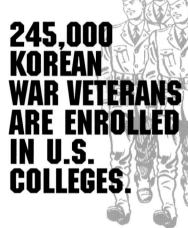

NO JOKING MATTER

Under threat of censorship from the State Subcommittee on Juvenile Delinquency, 26 American comic book publishers issue the Comics Code Authority. The code states that good must always triumph over evil and there will be no sympathetic treatment of criminals or undignified portrayal of law enforcement officers.

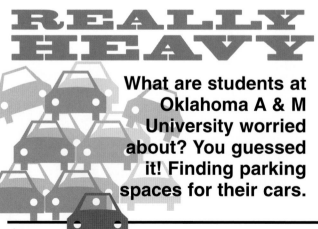

SheHero

Giddyup

YOU AND YOUR CAR...

NO OFF-COLOR JOKES

Tests conducted at the Iowa State College driving research laboratory show that tinted windshields impair vision.

Citing the over 2,500 traffic deaths annually due to the number of drivers who are red-green color-blind, Sun Chemical Corp. suggests a blue-yellow system be instituted.

The Better Vision Institute

concludes that distracted people drive best as evidenced by the higher number of accidents in the country versus reduction of accidents in cities, with accidents being very high on long, monotonous stretches of western roads.

If Only Men Drove Like Women

Records of reported accidents reveal that the average woman driver improves in skill from the age of 16 to 33 whereas most young men show a downward spiral in their skills until the age of 22.

Chicago's

traffic engineer announces that next year the city will boast the first radio-controlled traffic signals. A transmitter, installed on top of the Board of Trade Building, will send out radio impulses controlling the red and green lights.

Take A Deep Breath And Exhale

New York police begin city-wide use of the "drunkometer" with chemical test apparatus.

Smoke Gets In Your Eyes

A six-year research program conducted by the Stanford Research Institute concludes that the eye-burning smog that afflicts the Los Angeles area is caused by the chemical action of sunlight on auto exhaust fumes and industrial emissions.

A FEW REASONS FOR AUTOMOBILE ACCIDENTS
The Pennsylvania Department of Highways

RUGGED INDIVIDUALISM
UNHEALTHY DISRESPECT FOR THE LAW
LACK OF OPERATOR SKILL
LACK OF REGARD FOR HUMAN LIFE**

**Could be the result of three major wars within the last 35 years, hardening men to highway hazards.

A GENERAL ELECTRIC illuminating engineer makes the following prediction about what cars will look like in 50 years in the year 2004:

10 FUTURE FEATURES

- Headlights 10 times more powerful
- Fluorescent lamps that light the luggage compartment and engine
- Infrared lamps that clear windshields of ice and snow and interior condensation
- Illuminated instrument panels
- Fluorescent lamps, recessed in the bottoms of doors, that light automatically when the doors are opened
- Indicator lamps that light up to show trouble spots such as burned-out headlamp, low oil pressure, low oil level, high water temperature, etc.
- All four corners of the car illuminated by fluorescent tubes—red in the rear and amber in the front
- Turn signal and stop lamps brighter in the day
- A swivel-type dome spotlight that supplies a beam of light that will not interfere with the driver
- A "black light" that illuminates fluorescent knobs on switches and controls

But Officer, He Told Me To Make A Left Right Now

In Mexico City, a man flunks his driver's test when he runs over a traffic officer and breaks his leg.

1954 A HAIRY

If a woman's crowning glory is her hair, then her hairdresser is a king of hearts, who brings her reign into being.

Here in Portugal, the Hair Dressers' Guild of Lisbon has come up with a coiffure contest where 36 artists expose their masterpieces to the scrutiny of the judges.

Hairstylists from France and Spain as well as Portugal snip, clip, curry and comb to present these crowning moments to a waiting world.

CONTEST

1954

The judges review these creations.

Hairstyles are getting as distinctively different as dress styles, beribboned and bejeweled.

AND NOW FOR THE COIF THAT TOPS THEM ALL!

BUILDING AND CONSTRUCTION

Calling it an economic boost and a defense asset, President Eisenhower hails the opening of the N.Y. State Thruway.

President Eisenhower authorizes the construction of the St. Lawrence Seaway between Montreal and Lake Erie.

A GREAT MOMENT PRESERVED FOREVER

In Arlington, Virginia, sculptor **Felix de Weldon**'s new U.S. Marine Corps War Memorial, a giant bronze statue of the raising of the flag on Iwo Jima during World War II, is dedicated.

AT A COST OF $35 MILLION, THE DEFENSE DEPARTMENT COMPLETES CONSTRUCTION OF AN UNDERGROUND PENTAGON BENEATH RAVEN ROCK MOUNTAIN IN FREDERICK COUNTY, MARYLAND.

THESE FELLAS ARE ROCKS!

GIVING SOMETHING BACK
Laurance Spelman Rockefeller offers his 650-acre plantation on St. John, in the Virgin Islands, as a site for the first U.S. National Park in the Caribbean.

SAVING THE TREES FROM THE CHOPPING BLOCK
To save the trees from being cut down, **JOHN D. ROCKEFELLER JR.** donates $1 million to the state of California to help fund the purchase of the Calaveras South Grove redwoods in Tuolumne County.

The estate of the late **WILLIAM RANDOLPH HEARST** donates the publishing magnate's $25 million castle at San Simeon to the state of California, which declares the 303-acre grounds a public park.

WHAT A YEAR IT WAS!

DiGS

Archeologists in Egypt find Pharaoh Cheops' solar boat, opened to light after 4,700 years.

ONE WAY TO KEEP THOSE LiTTLE CROW'S-FEET AWAY

The mummy of a 10-year-old Inca girl preserved for more than 500 years is discovered in an icy tomb 20,000 feet up in the Chilean Andes.

GETTiNG A TOMB UP

A tomb believed to be that of Egyptian pharaoh Sankhet, who ruled about 2750 B.C., is discovered about 20 miles south of the Great Pyramid of Giza, and is believed to be the oldest known untouched tomb of a pharaoh.

THAT'S ONE OLD FOSSiL

Harvard University announces the discovery of fossils of primitive plants on the northern shore of Lake Superior dating back nearly two billion years.

Religion

LESS LATINUS CONFUSEUS

Pope gives permission to U.S. clergy to deliver sacraments in English.

NOW IF WE COULD JUST FIGURE OUT HOW TO GET THE WAFER

According to the Vatican, watching mass on television does not fill religious requirements for Catholics.

BE CAREFUL WHAT YOU DANCE FOR

Aborigines stage a rainmaking dance in Darwin, Australia as part of a native dance festival, but have to stop because of a downpour.

Barcelona opens its first synagogue since 1942.

Congregation Shearith Israel in New York celebrates the 300th anniversary of the first Jewish settlement in the U.S., founded in 1654 by 23 Jews.

SLIP, SLIDING AWAY

185,000 tons of rock, dirt and rubble fall into the Niagara River gorge after being dislodged from the top of Prospect Point, leaving a triangular chasm of about 70 feet.

How Low Can It Go?

Death Valley, California, the lowest spot in the Western Hemisphere, has sunk two additional feet since the last survey in 1937 and is now 281.9 feet below sea level.

How Deep Is The Ocean – How High Is The Sky

Using a bathyscaphe, two French naval officers set a new record for descent off the west coast of Africa at 13,287 feet, 88 feet more than 2 1/2 miles.

1954 SAN FRANCISCO
DOPE SMUGGLING RING
SMASHED

With the arrest of seven men in San Francisco, one of the largest dope smuggling rings of recent years is smashed.

The seized heroin and opium is the nucleus of what would have been a flood of narcotics worth millions on the national drug market.

Magazines with the centers cut out were used to conceal drugs worth hundreds of thousands. Much of the captured contraband was in the process of being prepared for distribution when seized by federal agents.

The illicit narcotics were smuggled into the country from Red China by way of Hong Kong, which federal agents say is one of the world's clearinghouses for opium from the Orient.

WHAT A YEAR IT WAS!

FOR SECRETARIES — 1555 *Shorthand*

FOR FINE GENERAL WRITING — 9556 *Fine writing*

FOR GENERAL OFFICE WORK — 1554 *Clerical*

FOR SALESMEN — 9460 *Carbon copies*

FOR SOCIAL CORRESPONDENCE — 9314M *Manuscript*

FOR BOOKKEEPERS — 2550 *Posting 1-2-3*

FOR GENERAL WRITING — 9668 *All Purpose*

FOR MUSIC WRITING — 9284 *Music*

FOR PITMAN SHORTHAND — 9128 *Shaded Writing*

FOR POSTING AND CHECKING — 9550 *Extra Fine*

FOR SCHOOL WORK (Educator Approved) — 1551 *Student*

FOR EXECUTIVES — 2284 *Signature Stub*

Give the pen with the right point for every writer

The gift for easier, more comfortable writing

DELUXE PUSH-PENCIL to match Deluxe Pens — *Regular and thin lead models*

DELUXE MODEL—Lustrous metal cap. Barrels in 5 solid colors

PUSH-PENCIL—to match Standard, Slender and Long Slender Pens

LONG SLENDER MODEL—Black and 5 smart colors

STANDARD MODEL—Black and 5 attractive colors

SLENDER MODEL—Black, white and 5 beautiful colors

PURSE MODEL—Choice of pastel colors

ONLY ESTERBROOK
gives you all these features

- Choice of more than 28 points
- 4 degrees of point flexibility
- 4 barrel styles—17 colors
- Writes instantly without pressure
- Never skips
- Fills from any ink bottle
- Uses any fountain pen ink
- Points instantly replaceable at any pen counter

POINT SELECTION INCLUDES MORE THAN 28 POINT STYLES • OR, YOU TRY A SALESMAN'S . . . NEXT, ALL POINTS INSTANTLY INTERCHANGEABLE—INSTANTLY RENEWABLE • IT'S SO EASY TO SELECT OR REPLACE

Esterbrook®

THE WORLD'S MOST PERSONAL FOUNTAIN PEN   FOUNTAIN PENS

CARRARA DESK PEN SET. This desk pen automatically fills itself from ink-fountain in base every time you return it to the socket. Fountain-base holds 40 times more ink than ordinary fountain pen. Pen takes your favorite Esterbrook point.

The Pen that fills itself

STANDARD POCKET SET. Esterbrook Fountain Pen and matching Push-Pencil. (Push the top to feed the lead.) Pencil holds 12 sticks of lead. Writes for months without reloading. Choice of regular or thin lead models.

DELUXE POCKET SET. Deluxe Esterbrook Pen with lustrous metal cap and matching Push-Pencil. Choice of aqua, midnight, sand, gray or maroon. Push-Pencil is available in two styles — for regular or thin leads.

COPYRIGHT 1954,
THE ESTERBROOK
PEN COMPANY

Esterbrook AMERICA'S PEN NAME SINCE 1858

55

1954

It's Not Always
BLACK & WHITE

The U.S. Supreme Court rules that "separate but equal" schools deny American citizens equal protection under the 14th Amendment.

IN THE COURTS

HOW ABOUT THE PARENTS' RIGHT TO PADDLE THE TEACHER?
The Alabama State Supreme Court turns down a $3,500 damage suit brought by an irate parent and rules that a schoolteacher has a right to paddle a pupil as long as he doesn't inflict excessive punishment.

HE DIDN'T EVEN CRACK A SMILE ON THIS ONE
Judge Gibson E. Gorman of Chicago Superior Court rules that a child born of artificial insemination is illegitimate if the donor is not the mother's husband and that the mother is guilty of adultery in such a case even though the insemination is by consent of her husband.

Twelve southern leaders agree not to comply with court integration order.

TO AVOID INTEGRATION, MISSISSIPPI VOTERS APPROVE ABOLITION OF PUBLIC SCHOOLS.

ALL-BLACK ARMED FORCES UNITS ARE ABOLISHED.

For the first time in history, the U.S. Supreme Court appoints the first black page boy, 14-year-old Charles Vernon Bush.

Despite anti-black demonstrations by 2,000 white students in Baltimore and Washington, local officials enforce racial desegregation.

Two southern gubernatorial candidates propose the ouster of the Supreme Court to preserve segregation.

And Now For Something Really New
All-black Fisk University in Nashville, Tennessee graduates its first white student since 1893.

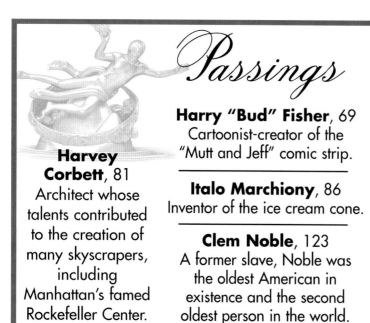

Passings

Harvey Corbett, 81
Architect whose talents contributed to the creation of many skyscrapers, including Manhattan's famed Rockefeller Center.

Harry "Bud" Fisher, 69
Cartoonist-creator of the "Mutt and Jeff" comic strip.

Italo Marchiony, 86
Inventor of the ice cream cone.

Clem Noble, 123
A former slave, Noble was the oldest American in existence and the second oldest person in the world.

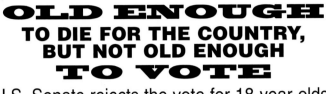

OLD ENOUGH TO DIE FOR THE COUNTRY, BUT NOT OLD ENOUGH TO VOTE

U.S. Senate rejects the vote for 18-year-olds.

ARMISTICE DAY,

the day set aside to commemorate World War I, is replaced by **VETERANS DAY**.

EVERYONE UNDER THE TABLE

Americans take part in the first nationwide civil defense test against atomic attack.

HOW ABOUT "CURRENT RESIDENT"?

Junk mail will no longer be delivered to "householder," according to the U.S. Post Office.

TO BREATHE OR NOT TO BREATHE – THAT IS THE QUESTION

Following 15 days of heavy smog, the governor of California shuts down Los Angeles oil refineries.

WHOOPS!

The U.S. Mint admits to the accidental release of three million rare Liberty Head silver dollars valued at $2 to $17 each.

BEWITCHED & BOTHERED BUT NOT BEWILDERED

Citing that it would be a blow to the tourist business, the Massachusetts Senate, by a vote of 17-10, refuses to go along with the state's House of Representatives in reversing the conviction of six Salem women who were hanged for witchcraft in 1692.

President Eisenhower proposes stripping convicted Communists of their U.S. citizenship.

President Eisenhower signs a bill adding the words **"under God"** to **"one nation indivisible"** in the Pledge of Allegiance.

President Eisenhower signs a bill that destroys the Communist Party as a political and legal entity in America.

Paving the way for private exploitation of nuclear power, President Eisenhower signs the Atomic Energy Act.

President Eisenhower signs bill extending Social Security to 10 million more people.

A Hot Time In The Old Town Tonight

With President Eisenhower in attendance, ground is broken in Pittsburgh for the first atomic power plant.

President Eisenhower

ARE YOU NOW OR HAVE YOU EVER BEEN?

McCARTHY HEARINGS ATTRACT MORE THAN 2,000 PEOPLE A DAY WHO CRAM THE SENATE CAUCUS ROOM.

CBS newsman **Edward R. Murrow** takes on the senator from Wisconsin, accusing McCarthy of engaging in half-truths and confusing the public about the internal and external threats of Communism.

The Atomic Energy Commission declares nuclear scientist **J. Robert Oppenheimer** a security risk, and the man who led the wartime effort to develop the atomic bomb is suspended.

COULD BE A SHOCKING EXPERIENCE
U.S. Congress institutes death penalty for espionage in peacetime.

LONE VOICE OF REASON IN THE WILDERNESS

With Senator Fulbright casting the only dissenting vote, the U.S. Senate votes $214,000 for the Joseph R. McCarthy investigation of alleged Communists in the government.

McCARTHY CHARGES THAT COMMUNISTS HAVE INFILTRATED THE CIA AND ATOMIC PLANTS.

The Army-McCarthy hearings end with the Army maintaining that McCarthy and his chief counsel, 27-year-old Roy M. Cohn, sought preferential treatment for Pvt. G. David Schine, a subcommittee investigator before he was drafted.

Senate begins inquiry into the clash between the U.S. Army and McCarthy.

The U.S. Senate votes 67-22 to condemn Joseph R. McCarthy for conduct unbecoming a Senator.

Joseph R. McCarthy

Crimes & Misdemeanors 1954

IT'S CALLED A FLYING HEADLOCK

A professional wrestler is arrested in Wichita, Kansas after settling an argument by tossing her husband through the bedroom window.

HE'S OFF TO JAIL, CHA CHA CHA

Busted by FBI agents for a Chicago bank robbery, Samuel Hochstetler tells the agents that he spent $5,000 of the $31,000 haul on dance lessons and is now quite proficient in the fox trot, waltz, rhumba, mambo, tango and samba.

CRIME DOESN'T PAY – BUT YOU DO

FBI Director J. Edgar Hoover, testifying before the House Appropriations Committee, states that crime costs each American family an average of $495 a year.

Convicted kidnapper and rapist, 32-year-old Caryl Chessman, receives a stay of execution the day before he is scheduled to die in San Quentin's gas chamber.

A scoutmaster in Perrysburg, Ohio is fined $50 for waving a sign reading "Speed Trap Ahead."

THE GREAT ESCAPE

STRIKE THREE AND YOU'RE OUT – REALLY OUT

Prison guards halt a baseball game in Alabama between Atmore State Prison and Kilby Prison when they discover that 19 convicts had escaped through a steel-mesh fence.

PUTTING A HICCUP INTO HIS CAPTURE

After sticking up a service station attendant and a cab driver in El Sobrante, California, a creative crook gave each of his victims a bottle of whiskey, instructing them to chug-a-lug it in six minutes, thus making it difficult for them to decide if he went this-a-way or that-a-way.

AT LEAST THEY SAID THANK YOU

Following is the note left for Jail Superintendent James Hammond by two prisoners who escaped from the county jail's paddy wagon:

Dear Jim,

Sorry to eat and run, but we have to catch a train.

FOREIGN AFFAIRS

Vietnam

First U.S. ship arrives in Haiphong to evacuate refugees to South Vietnam.

SOMETIMES HOME IS NO PLACE TO BE HOME

In a grand exodus, over 250,000 North Vietnamese leave their Communist-controlled homeland for South Vietnam.

Puerto Rican fanatics open fire on the floor

of the House of Representatives injuring five congressmen: Alvin M. Bentley, Ben F. Jensen, George H. Fallon, Kenneth A. Roberts and Clifford Davis.

The four Puerto Ricans involved in the shooting of five congressmen are sentenced in Washington, D.C. to maximum jail terms.

THAT WAS A LOT OF HUDDLED MASSES

Ellis Island, the "gateway to America" for over 20 million immigrants, closes down after 62 years.

Switzerland

THEY'RE ALL TICKED OFF

Protesting against U.S. hike in watch tariffs, 3,000 Swiss watchmakers stage a protest, with some shop-keepers refusing to sell American cigarettes, nylons or Coca-Cola.

France

FASTER THAN A SPEEDING...

Powered by an electric locomotive, a French train hits a new record traveling speed of an unprecedented 151 mph.

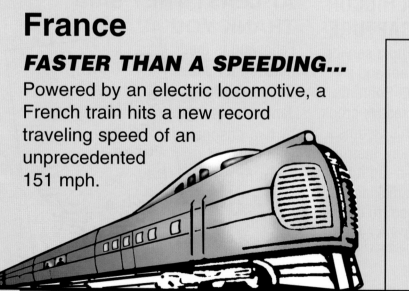

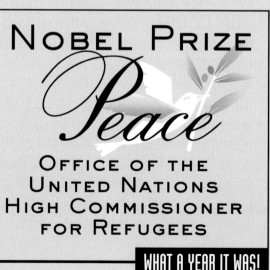

NOBEL PRIZE

Peace

OFFICE OF THE UNITED NATIONS HIGH COMMISSIONER FOR REFUGEES

WHAT A YEAR IT WAS!

TRYING TO EXTINGUISH THE SMOKING GUN

14 major tobacco companies create a Tobacco Industry Research Committee to counter scientific reports linking lung cancer to smoking.

LIGHTENING
HER LOAD ALONG THE WAY

In labor and en route to the hospital in Ludington, Michigan, a young woman delivers her triplets as follows: Tom in the car, Dick in a hospital elevator and last, but not least, Harry in the delivery room.

NOT THAT SAME OLD TUNE AGAIN

A University of Chicago scholar asserts that birds that sing the same song repeatedly are in danger of getting bored with their singing.

AND LET THERE BE LIGHT — AND THERE WAS

The U.S. holds the #1 position in world power production, with 98% of its population currently hooked up to electric lines.

TRIPPING THE LIGHT FANTASTIC

New York celebrates the 75th anniversary of Edison's light-bulb by lighting a 75,000-watt bulb at Rockefeller Center.

LOOK, THE SKY IS FALLING

The U.S. Air Force gives Mrs. Hewlett Hodges the eight-pound meteorite that struck and injured her when it fell from the sky.

THE DARKER, THE TASTIER

The National Research Council reports that the average consumer says orange juice tastes better when it is a dark orange color rather than when it's a lemon color.

MORE POWER THAN A PISTOL

The U.S. Army announces that two new weapons capable of using either atomic or conventional warheads are being delivered to troops for tactical support of ground fighting.

STRING BEAN CAPITAL OF THE WORLD

A Harvard anthropologist reports that America is raising too many tall and skinny people.

CHALK ONE UP FOR LOVE

Salem, Oregon's state unemployment compensation commission rules that a woman who quits her job so she can spend more time with her fiancé is entitled to unemployment benefits.

HURRICANE – THY NAME BE WOMAN

Starting with the letter "A," the U.S. Weather Service commences use of female names for hurricanes.

A STINKY SUBJECT

A 72-year-old housewife in Mineola, New York is seeking a separation from her husband, charging that he has refused to bathe during their 12 years of marriage.

THAT'S WHAT YOU GET FOR FALLING ASLEEP AT THE TABLE

A Boston woman is seeking annulment of her marriage on the grounds that after she dozed off at her wedding reception, she awoke to find that the groom and guests had all left and she didn't see her husband again for five years.

I GUESS THEY DIDN'T HEAR THE PHRASE "DON'T EVER TAKE A WOODEN EGG"

Experiments conducted with a flock of wild herring gulls by the zoology department at the University of Groningen in the Netherlands reveal that mother birds prefer to sit on artificial wooden eggs rather than the ones they laid themselves.

Oh My Aching Tootsies

The average person takes about 14,080 steps daily and a 200-pound man puts a daily workload of 1,408,000 pounds or 704 tons on each foot.

1954

UP, UP & AWAY

BOEING CONDUCTS INITIAL FLIGHT OF A B-52A BOMBER.

Reaching a cruising speed of 600 mph, Boeing launches the *Dash Eighty*, a prototype of a model to be called 707, which is designed for intercontinental travel and can hold up to 219 passengers.

THE U.S. AIR FORCE AUTHORIZES THE FIRST SUPERSONIC BOMBER, THE B-58.

COME FLY WITH ME

President Eisenhower authorizes creation of the U.S. Air Force Academy in Colorado.

UP, UP & REALLY AWAY, IN MY BEAUTIFUL BALLOON

The USAF Air Weather Service releases a weather balloon that rises 26 miles, 110 times the height of the Empire State Building.

Hey, Did Ya Get A Glimpse Of Santa?

Scandinavian Airlines establishes the first regularly scheduled flight over the North Pole flying from Los Angeles to Copenhagen.

A CHILLING EXPERIENCE

Two U.S. icebreakers complete the first transit of the Northwest Passage through McClure Strait.

Trenton, New Jersey becomes the first major American city with a downtown passenger heliport.

Automatic toll collectors are installed on the New Jersey Turnpike.

The Little Trains That Couldn't

Santa Fe retires its last steam engine, becoming the biggest completely dieselized U.S. railroad, with 1,622 diesel units.

As tall as a 25-story building and costing $197,869,000, the U.S. Navy launches the 1,046-foot FORRESTAL, the largest aircraft carrier in the world.

New Words & Expressions

1954

Goof
An error.

Atomic Rain
Radioactive fallout from atomic bomb explosions.

Cat Music
Music with a good dancing beat, often with interesting lyrics.

Cha-Cha-Cha
A fashionable Cuban dance.

One-Take
A movie scene that is shot only one time.

COLORED
WHITES ONLY

Resegregate
To segregate a school that has already been desegregated.

Belt
To sing with gusto.

Softback
A soft-cover book.

SPECTACULAR
A lavish television show with lots of entertainment.

Biddy Basketball
Basketball for little kids.

Crazy Pants
Groovy, colorful, slender pants for teens.

Speedwalk
A sidewalk that moves.

Tollway
A toll highway.

Dragster
A hot-rod car.

Video-Pool Pickup
Footage shot by one network or station then shown on others.

YOUR BRAIN

Brainprint
Pictures of brainwaves.

Duoscopic
A specially formatted television set that can display two shows at the same time.

Windfall Profits
Exceptionally high profits.

Bricabracomaniac
A person who really likes bric-a-brac.

WHAT A YEAR IT WAS!

63

"Bill thinks of the nicest things. He gave me an extension telephone for the kitchen and one for the bedroom too."

"Thanks ever so much, son, for the extension telephone. It's a big comfort to have it close by in my bedroom."

HERE'S SOMETHING NEW

AND DIFFERENT FOR CHRISTMAS

Give an extension telephone to someone you love

Have you been searching for something new and different in a Christmas gift? Something that is distinctive, yet practical, and will last the whole year through?

You couldn't do better than an extension telephone for Mother or Dad, son or daughter, or Grandma and Grandpa. For 365 days and nights it will save steps, time and effort. And it's mighty handy, too, in an emergency.

If you'll order in time we'll do our best to install the extension telephone before Christmas.

If that isn't possible, we'll deliver the telephone, attractively wrapped, so you can put it under the tree with the other gifts. Then we'll come around after Christmas and install it in bedroom, living room, or kitchen, or wherever you wish.

The cost is small—just pennies a day for each extension telephone. Just call the business office of your local Bell telephone company.

 BELL TELEPHONE SYSTEM

"My wife sure knows how to pick out the right Christmas gifts. Gave me an extension telephone for my hobby room downstairs."

"You'll never guess what Dad gave me! A telephone of my very own— right in my room!"

Arts & ENTERTAINMENT

MOVIES

JACK LEMMON makes his film debut in *Phffft!* co-starring **JUDY HOLLIDAY**.

KIM NOVAK gets her first major roles as a gun moll who seduces **FRED MACMURRAY** in *Pushover* and as Jack Lemmon's problematic girlfriend in *Phffft!*

MUSIC

NAT KING COLE signs a two-year exclusive contract with the Sands Hotel, becoming the first black performer to break the Las Vegas color barrier.

TELEVISION

AND HERE'S STEVO

A local success, **STEVE ALLEN** moves his *Tonight!* show to an NBC national slot.

DANCE

A Midsummer Night's Dream opens at the Metropolitan Opera House with **MOIRA SHEARER** as Titania.

What's Playing AT THE MOVIES

Brigadoon
BRINGING UP MOTHER
BROKEN LANCE
The Caine Mutiny
Carmen Jones
THE COUNTRY GIRL
THE DAM BUSTERS
Deep In My Heart
Devil Girl From Mars
Dial M For Murder
DOCTOR IN THE HOUSE
DRAGNET
The Egyptian
ELEPHANT WALK
EXECUTIVE SUITE
The Fast And The Furious
Francis Joins The WACs
The French Line
Garden Of Eden
GARDEN OF EVIL
THE GLENN MILLER STORY
HAPPILY EVER AFTER
The High And The Mighty

20,000 Leagues Under The Sea
A STAR IS BORN
The Adventures Of Robinson Crusoe
ANIMAL FARM
AN INSPECTOR CALLS
The Barefoot Contessa
BEACHHEAD
Beau Brummell
BEWITCHED BUNNY
THE BOB MATHIAS STORY
THE BOUNTY HUNTER
THE BOWERY BOYS MEET THE MONSTERS

HOBSON'S CHOICE
It Should Happen To You
Johnny Guitar
KING RICHARD AND THE CRUSADERS
LA STRADA
The Last Time I Saw Paris
The Long, Long Trailer
MA AND PA KETTLE AT HOME
MAD ABOUT MEN
THE MAD MAGICIAN
Magnificent Obsession
Men Of The Fighting Lady
THE NAKED JUNGLE
On The Waterfront
OUT OF THIS WORLD
THE OUTCAST
PHFFFT!
PRINCE VALIANT
PRISONER OF WAR
PRIVATE EYE POPEYE
THE PURPLE PLAIN
PUSHOVER

REAR WINDOW
RED GARTERS
RIOT IN CELL BLOCK 11
RIVER OF NO RETURN
Rogue Cop
Romeo And Juliet
ROSE MARIE
SABRINA
SALT OF THE EARTH
Seven Brides For Seven Brothers
SEVEN SAMURAI
THE SILVER CHALICE
THE STUDENT PRINCE
SUDDENLY
Susan Slept Here
TARGET EARTH
THEM!
There's No Business Like Show Business
Three Coins In The Fountain
VALLEY OF THE KINGS
Vera Cruz
WHITE CHRISTMAS

The red carpet is out at International Airport in Miami, Florida for film star **Jimmy Stewart** and his wife, **Gloria**, as they arrive for the world premiere of Jimmy's latest picture, *The Glenn Miller Story.*

Now playing at three theaters, the Miracle, the Miami and the Carib, the premiere is one of the top events of the winter season.

Winter vacationists and natives of the Florida resort city jam all three theaters and the streets to catch a glimpse of the popular Jimmy and his missus.

WELCOME TO MIAMI

Civic officials and Air Force reserve officers greet the World War II bomber pilot, who plays the part of the heroic bandleader in the Technicolor musical biography.

Universal International executives are on hand for the ceremonies honoring a top Hollywood star.

WHAT A YEAR IT WAS!

Movie Stars in São Paulo

Hollywood couple **Barbara Rush** and **Jeffrey Hunter** get in a bit of sight-seeing before attending São Paulo's first motion picture festival.

Fans in front of the Morocco, São Paulo's largest theater, are rewarded as **Irene Dunne** *(above)* heads the parade of luminaries to view top motion pictures of the year.

Starlet **Barbara Rush** and **Jeffrey Hunter** make their bow to Brazil's international movie event.

Stage and screen musical comedy star **Ann Miller** is another São Paulo guest *(above)*, followed by a veteran of countless productions, **Walter Pidgeon** *(below)*.

1954

The Academy Awards

"And The Winner Is..."

Oscars® Presented in 1954

BEST PICTURE
FROM HERE TO ETERNITY

BEST ACTOR
WILLIAM HOLDEN, *Stalag 17*

BEST ACTRESS
AUDREY HEPBURN, *Roman Holiday*

BEST DIRECTOR
FRED ZINNEMANN,
From Here To Eternity

Audrey Hepburn

BEST SUPPORTING ACTOR
FRANK SINATRA, *From Here To Eternity*

BEST SUPPORTING ACTRESS
DONNA REED, *From Here To Eternity*

BEST SONG
"SECRET LOVE," *Calamity Jane*

Within a few days, Audrey Hepburn wins an Academy Award for *Roman Holiday* and a Tony Award for *Ondine*.

1954 Favorites *(Oscars® Presented in 1955)*

BEST PICTURE
ON THE WATERFRONT

BEST ACTOR
MARLON BRANDO,
On The Waterfront

Grace Kelly

BEST ACTRESS
GRACE KELLY, *The Country Girl*

BEST DIRECTOR
ELIA KAZAN,
On The Waterfront

BEST SUPPORTING ACTOR
EDMOND O'BRIEN, *The Barefoot Contessa*

BEST SUPPORTING ACTRESS
EVA MARIE SAINT, *On The Waterfront*

BEST SONG
"THREE COINS IN THE FOUNTAIN,"
Three Coins In The Fountain

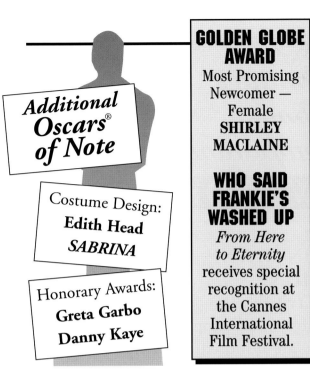

Additional Oscars® of Note

Costume Design:
Edith Head
SABRINA

Honorary Awards:
Greta Garbo
Danny Kaye

GOLDEN GLOBE AWARD

Most Promising Newcomer — Female
SHIRLEY MACLAINE

WHO SAID FRANKIE'S WASHED UP

From Here to Eternity receives special recognition at the Cannes International Film Festival.

PAYCHECKS

Spencer Tracy

Spencer Tracy earns $165,000 for his role in *Broken Lance*.

Audrey Hepburn scores $15,000 for her role in *Sabrina*.

HOW'S A GIRL TO MAKE ENDS MEET ON THIS?

Citing that she is underpaid earning only $1,250 a week, **Marilyn Monroe** refuses to show up for work and flies off to Japan with her husband, **Joe DiMaggio**.

TOP-GROSSING FILM OF THE YEAR

White Christmas

Starring Bing Crosby, Danny Kaye, Rosemary Clooney & Vera-Ellen

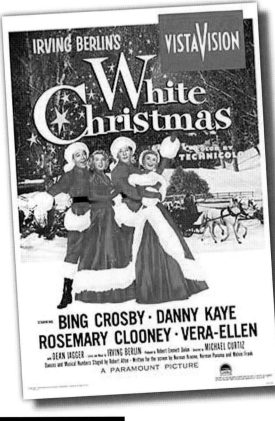

Dorothy Dandridge receives $18,000 for her appearance in *Carmen Jones*.

Jayne Mansfield

Jayne Mansfield arrives in Los Angeles and enrolls in acting classes at UCLA.

Michael Kidd choreographs *Seven Brides for Seven Brothers*, said to be one of the most robust and dazzling displays of dance ever seen on film.

Roger Moore is offered contracts with both the Royal Shakespeare Company and MGM. **Noel Coward** advises him to go for the money.

François Truffaut directs his first short film.

HIS CUP DIDN'T RUNNETH OVER

Paul Newman makes his first screen appearance as the star of a biblical epic, *The Silver Chalice*.

FRANKLY, HE'S MOVING ON

53-year-old **Clark Gable**, veteran of 23 years at MGM, announces that he will not be renewing his contract with the studio as he plans to freelance and maybe try directing.

Woman's Home Companion AWARDS

JOHN WAYNE and JUNE ALLYSON, two of Hollywood's top stars, are honored by *Woman's Home Companion*. Miss Allyson receives her award for her outstanding work in *The Glenn Miller Story*.

The distinction comes to the two actors as the result of a poll taken throughout the nation where women of America render their verdict on the efforts of moviemakers and their stars.

— PASSINGS —

John Balderston, 64

Reporter-turned-author-turned-screenwriter who wrote or co-wrote such movies as *Gone with the Wind*, *The Prisoner of Zenda* and *The Lives of a Bengal Lancer* and adapted *The Last of the Mohicans* and *Gaslight*.

Lionel Barrymore, 76

Barrymore

A member of one of history's most revered acting families (the Drews and the Barrymores), Lionel was a veteran of the theater, radio and movies. Throughout his long career he acted alongside his grandmother Mrs. John Drew, as well as his siblings, John and Ethel. He won an Academy Award for his performance in *A Free Soul*. Barrymore starred in many films, including *David Copperfield*, *Treasure Island* and *Dinner At Eight*. Later in life he played Scrooge yearly on a radio version of *A Christmas Carol*.

Sydney Greenstreet, 74

Greenstreet

Best known for his roles in *Casablanca* and *The Maltese Falcon*, Greenstreet was a success on stage long before he became famous on the silver screen.

Dr. Auguste Lumière, 91

Along with brother Louis, Lumière was co-inventor of the movie camera and projector.

WHAT A YEAR IT WAS!

73

BIG BUCKS
AT THE BOX OFFICE

Marlon Brando
Gary Cooper
Bing Crosby
William Holden
Alan Ladd
Dean Martin & Jerry Lewis
Marilyn Monroe
James Stewart
John Wayne
Jane Wyman

Marilyn Monroe

Dean Martin & Jerry Lewis

STARS
OF TOMORROW

Suzan Ball
Richard Burton
Pat Crowley
Audrey Hepburn
Grace Kelly
Guy Madison
Maggie McNamara
Cameron Mitchell
Aldo Ray
Elaine Stewart

Jane Wyman

Gary Cooper

Famous
BIRTHS

Jim Belushi
James Cameron
Jane Campion
Joel Coen
Lesley-Anne Down
Amy Heckerling
Ron Howard
Ang Lee
Anthony Minghella
Michael Moore
Rick Moranis
Dennis Quaid
Kathleen Quinlan
Rene Russo
John Travolta
Kathleen Turner
Denzel Washington

Elaine Stewart

WHAT A YEAR IT WAS!

All's Almost Empty On The Set

The movie set of Lady Godiva of Coventry is cleared of all but essential personnel in preparation for MAUREEN O'HARA to shoot the most famous naked horseback ride in history.

MAY THIS TOO, TOO SOLID FLESH MOVE BLITHELY ACROSS THE DEEPEST CORNERS OF THE STAGE

Sir Laurence Olivier practices twirling a cane and a little soft shoe for his debut as a song-and-dance man in an upcoming benefit show.

LINDY'S HOP INTO THE MOVIES

Charles Lindbergh has just sold the movie rights to his best-selling book *The Spirit of St. Louis* for a record $1,000,000.

RKO Pictures' board of directors approves **Howard Hughes'** offer to buy out all other stockholders.

MGM's pension program for veteran employees, including its stars, goes into effect this year starting March 1st.

The White House announces that actor **Robert Montgomery** is now on the presidential staff as a special adviser in visual communications.

SCORE ONE FOR FREEDOM OF SPEECH!

A grand jury in Elizabeth, New Jersey rejects efforts to ban the film **THE MOON IS BLUE** as obscene.

Ohio's Film Censorship Division authorizes exhibition of these formerly banned films: **THE MOON IS BLUE, THE OUTLAW, WAYS OF LOVE, KISS TOMORROW GOODBYE** and **MOM AND DAD**.

The U.S. Supreme Court overrules New York's ban on the French film **LA RONDE**.

The New York Censor Board reverses itself and authorizes Walt Disney's **VANISHING PRAIRIE** to be shown with a two-minute sequence of the birth of a buffalo calf.

FIRST: "FRANKLY, MY DEAR, I DON'T GIVE A DAMN"

"Go to hell" breaks another screen taboo against swear words when it is part of the dialogue in **On the Waterfront**.

Jane Russell in **The Outlaw**

Kodak
TRADE-MARK

Sunny memories for keeps in vacation snapshots

A few pennies—a few seconds —that's all it takes! You've caught the golden hours to enjoy all over again.

Help Others to Health— GIVE BLOOD NOW!

Have your camera with you everywhere—for that's where great snapshots are. Around home. On that special occasion. On family outings and vacations. Wherever you are, wherever you go. Then you'll *save* all those wonderful memories instead of *wishing* you had.

Big, brilliant "preview" finder on this Kodak Duaflex III Camera shows you your picture big and clear before you snap. With Kodet Lens, $14.95, including Federal Tax. Flasholder, $4.

Ever miss a priceless snapshot because the film ran out? With the new, thrifty Duo-Pak, you have 2 rolls of Kodak Film—one for your camera, one for a spare. And there's a nice little saving, too. In the popular 620, 120, and 127 sizes. (All Kodak Films come in single rolls, too.)

First choice of beginners and experts alike— Genuine Kodak Film—*in the familiar yellow box*

Eastman Kodak Company, Rochester 4, N.Y.

Hey Mom, What's On TV Tonight?

The Adventures Of Kit Carson
The Adventures Of Ozzie And Harriet
The Adventures Of Superman
The Adventures Of Wild Bill Hickok
Armstrong Circle Theatre
Arthur Godfrey's Talent Scouts*
The Arthur Murray Party
Beat The Clock
The Big Story
Big Town
Break The Bank
The Burns And Allen Show
Cavalcade Of America
The Colgate Comedy Hour*
Death Valley Days
The Dinah Shore Show
Doctor I.Q.
Douglas Fairbanks, Jr., Presents
Dragnet*
Fireside Theatre
Flash Gordon
Ford Theatre
Four Star Playhouse
The Gene Autry Show
Howdy Doody

I Married Joan
I've Got A Secret
The Jack Benny Show
The Jackie Gleason Show*
The Jane Froman Show
Kukla, Fran & Ollie
Life Begins At Eighty
The Life Of Riley
The Lone Ranger
The Loretta Young Show
Lux Video Theatre
Make Room For Daddy
Mama
Man Against Crime
Masquerade Party
Meet Millie
Meet The Press
The Milton Berle Show*
Motorama*
Mr. Peepers
My Favorite Husband
My Little Margie
Name That Tune
Omnibus
Our Miss Brooks
Pantomime Quiz
The Perry Como Show
Person To Person

Private Secretary
Ramar Of The Jungle
The Ray Bolger Show
The Ray Milland Show
The Red Skelton Show
Robert Montgomery Presents
The Sammy Kaye Show
See It Now
Stop The Music
The Stork Club
Studio One
Suspense
Ted Mack's Original Amateur Hour
This Is Your Life*
Toast Of The Town
Topper
Treasury Men In Action
Truth Or Consequences
Twenty Questions
Voice Of Firestone
The Walter Winchell Show
What's My Line?
You Are There
You Asked For It
You Bet Your Life*
Your Hit Parade

The Adventures of Rin Tin Tin

Annie Oakley

The Best In Mystery

The Best Of Broadway

Caesar's Hour

Climax

Davy Crockett

December Bride

Disneyland

The Donald O'Connor Texaco Show

Father Knows Best

Jimmy Durante

The George Gobel Show

The Gloria Swanson Show

The Imogene Coca Show

The Jimmy Durante Show

The Jo Stafford Show

The Johnny Otis Show

Lassie

The Lineup

Medic

The Mickey Rooney Show

People Are Funny

Producers' Showcase

The Public Defender

Shower Of Stars

The Spike Jones Show

Studio 57

That's My Boy

Tonight!

The Tony Martin Show

The Fred Waring Show

The George Jessel Show

The Goldbergs

Kay Kyser's College Of Musical Knowledge

Mr. & Mrs. North

My Friend Irma

Paul Whiteman's TV Teen Club

The RCA Victor Show

Saturday Night Revue

Your Show Of Shows

Sid Caesar

Spike Jones

Bud Abbott
Eddie Albert
Fred Allen
Steve Allen
Morey Amsterdam
Eve Arden
Jim Backus
John Barrymore Jr.
Orson Bean
Ralph Bellamy
Polly Bergen
Sid Caesar
Kitty Carlisle
Art Carney
Johnny Carson
Leo G. Carroll
Pat Carroll
Jackie Coogan
Alistair Cooke
Lou Costello
Richard Crenna
Walter Cronkite
Hume Cronyn
Arlene Dahl
Don DeFore
Jimmy Dorsey
Tommy Dorsey
Ralph Edwards
Faye Emerson
Nanette Fabray
Tennessee Ernie Ford
Merv Griffin
June Havoc
Boris Karloff
Ernie Kovacs

Jimmy & Tommy Dorsey

Eve Arden

George Reeves

Jack Webb

Natalie Wood

Peter Lawford
Jerry Lewis
Art Linkletter
Dean Martin
Groucho Marx
Walter Matthau
Audrey Meadows
Jayne Meadows
Sidney Miller
Martin Milner
Elizabeth Montgomery
Edward R. Murrow
Ricky Nelson
Bert Parks
Jane Pickens
Tony Randall
Ronald Reagan
George Reeves
Carl Reiner
Cliff Robertson
Cesar Romero
Eric Sevareid
Ann Sothern
Gale Storm
Ralph Story
Elaine Stritch
Jessica Tandy
Dick Van Patten
Mike Wallace
Jack Warden
Jack Webb
Marie Wilson
Natalie Wood
Fay Wray
Martha Wright

BOY, WAS HER FACE RED

During a live broadcast, **Betty Furness** has a humiliating experience as she tries unsuccessfully to open a Westinghouse refrigerator door.

In the first nationally televised beauty pageant, 19-year-old **Lee Ann Meriwether** is named Miss America 1955.

GOING TO THE DOGS

The great-great-great-grandson of the original **Rin Tin Tin** is one of several German shepherds playing the lead in the popular television program.

Married acting couple **Hume Cronyn** and **Jessica Tandy** star in both the radio and television versions of *The Marriage*.

CBS' *Climax* drama anthology presents the first James Bond movie, *Casino Royale*, starring **Barry Nelson** in the title role with **Peter Lorre** playing a Soviet agent.

ABC pays $50,000 per episode for *Disneyland*, a **Walt Disney** television series. The first episode of *Davy Crockett* airs in December, with **Fess Parker** costumed in buckskins and a coonskin hat.

"DER BINGLE" CROONS ON THE TUBE
Bing Crosby appears in his first television special.

Ted Mack's *Original Amateur Hour* begins broadcasting in color.

President Eisenhower conducts the first televised Cabinet meeting.

The eight-nation Eurovision network is launched with a telecast from the Vatican.

Now in its second season, *General Electric Theater* hires **Ronald Reagan** as its host.

To compete with NBC's *Today* show, CBS launches *The Morning Show* with **Walter Cronkite**.

EMMY awards

Television profits exceed radio profits for the first time.

RCA begins mass production of color televisions with 12″ screen for under $1,000.

SERIES

Situation Comedy
Make Room For Daddy

Dramatic
The U.S. Steel Hour

Variety
Disneyland

Mystery or Intrigue
Dragnet

Children's Program
Lassie

Best Direction
"Twelve Angry Men"
Studio One
Franklin Schaffner

Best Written Dramatic Material
"Twelve Angry Men"
Studio One
Reginald Rose

PERFORMERS

Actor   **Danny Thomas**
Make Room For Daddy

Actress   **Loretta Young**
The Loretta Young Show

Supporting Actor   **Art Carney**
The Jackie Gleason Show

Supporting Actress   **Audrey Meadows**
The Jackie Gleason Show

Most Outstanding New Personality
George Gobel

June Lockhart & Lassie

Loretta Young

Art Carney

1954

The Bing Crosby Show

Crime Classics

Dragnet

Gunsmoke

The Edgar Bergen-Charlie McCarthy Show

Fibber McGee & Molly

Lone Ranger

Molle Mystery Theatre

What's Playing On The RADIO

Sherlock Holmes

Mr. Keen, Tracer of Lost Persons

Whistler

Yours Truly, Johnny Dollar

TOP RATED EVENING
RADIO PROGRAMS
(WINTER SCHEDULE)

Amos 'n' Andy
The Jack Benny Show
People Are Funny
Lux Radio Theatre
My Little Margie
Our Miss Brooks
Walk A Mile
Mr. & Mrs. North
Suspense
You Bet Your Life

TOP RATED DAYTIME
RADIO PROGRAMS

Our Gal Sunday
The Romance Of Helen Trent
The Guiding Light
Arthur Godfrey's Talent Scouts
Wendy Warren And The News
This Is Nora Drake
Aunt Jenny's Real Life Stories

Richard Buckley's group buys N.Y. radio station WNEW for more than $2 million.

NUMBER OF RADIO STATIONS WORLDWIDE
8,000
NUMBER OF RADIOS IN U.S. HOMES
45,020,000, or 94.7% of all U.S. households

WHEN AMERICA SPEAKS, THEY LISTEN

VOICE OF AMERICA broadcasts daily in 34 languages, with 77% of the total output directed to the Soviet bloc.

HELLO, THIS IS MARS CALLING— SO WHAT'S NEW?

The Commonwealth Scientific & Industrial Organization of Australia is given a grant by the Carnegie Corporation to investigate mysterious radio beams reaching the earth from outer space.

NBC announces the disbandment of the NBC Symphony Orchestra to be replaced by the Boston Symphony under the direction of **Charles Munch**.

ENDING THE YEAR ON A HIGH NOTE

Great Britain's BBC radio broadcasts performances of three new operas: **The Turn of the Screw** by **Benjamin Britten**, **Nelson** by **Lennox Berkeley** and **Troilus and Cressida** by **William Walton**.

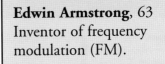
FAMOUS BIRTH — **Howard Stern**

THE END OF OLD FAVORITES

The Bob Hope Show
The Falcon
Let's Pretend
The Shadow
Sky King
Stars Over Hollywood
Twenty Questions

Bob Hope

PASSINGS

Edwin Armstrong, 63 Inventor of frequency modulation (FM).

Claude Hooper, 56 Created a way to find out the success of radio —and later television— shows, known as Hooper Ratings.

Slumber party? Gee, that's dandy!
Look your sharpest, everyone!
Snappy PJ's come in handy —
"Fresh up" parties sure are fun!

Copyright 1954 by The Seven-Up Company

"Fresh up" with Seven-Up!

THE ALL-FAMILY DRINK! Enjoy sparkling, crystal-clear 7-Up . . . often. Seven-Up is so pure, so good, so wholesome that everybody — from tiny tots to grandmas and all ages in between — may "fresh up" to his heart's content. And 7-Up makes *food* taste *extra* good. So have a Stackwich with chilled 7-Up. Buy 7-Up wherever you see those bright 7-Up signs. **You like it . . . it likes you!**

Get a family supply of 24 bottles. Buy 7-Up by the case. Or get the handy 7-Up Family Pack. Easy-lift center handle, easy to store.

84

POPULAR MUSIC

CAN BLUE SUEDE SHOES BE FAR BEHIND?

To celebrate turning 19, an unknown singer named ELVIS PRESLEY pays $4.00 at a Memphis studio to record *Careless Love* and *I'll Never Stand in Your Way.*

Sun Records releases ELVIS PRESLEY'S first record—*That's All Right (Mama)* and *Blue Moon of Kentucky*—and BILLBOARD calls him "a strong new talent."

ELVIS PRESLEY makes a commercial for SOUTHERN MADE DOUGHNUTS and sings the jingle.

NEW RECORDING ARTISTS

LaVern Baker

Sammy Davis Jr.

The McGuire Sisters

The Platters

Elvis Presley

Andy Williams

Americans buy a record 225 million recordings and for the first time, 78s account for less than 50% of revenues. **Mercury** and **RCA Victor** discontinue sending 78 rpm demos to radio stations.

With two big hits, 26-year-old **Eddie Fisher** is the nation's No. 1 singing idol.

HE DEFINITELY HAS THE WORLD ON A STRING

Overcoming predictions of the end of his career, **Frank Sinatra's** recording of *Young at Heart* is high on the charts along with three other songs.

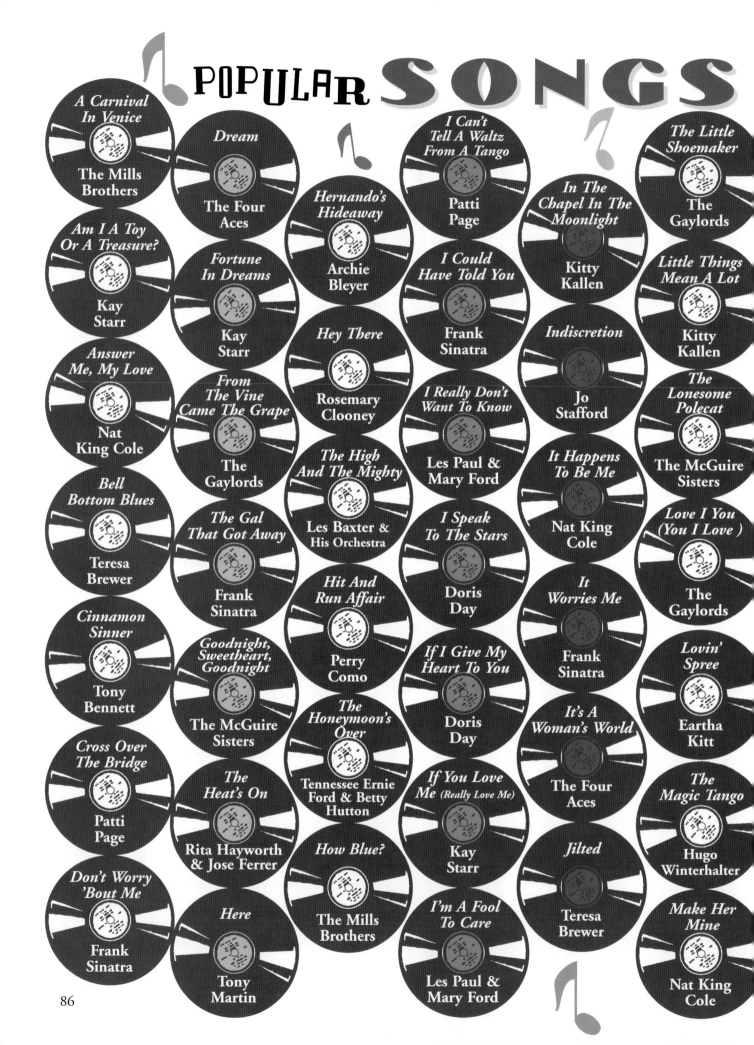

POPULAR SONGS

A Carnival In Venice — The Mills Brothers

Am I A Toy Or A Treasure? — Kay Starr

Answer Me, My Love — Nat King Cole

Bell Bottom Blues — Teresa Brewer

Cinnamon Sinner — Tony Bennett

Cross Over The Bridge — Patti Page

Don't Worry 'Bout Me — Frank Sinatra

Dream — The Four Aces

Fortune In Dreams — Kay Starr

From The Vine Came The Grape — The Gaylords

The Gal That Got Away — Frank Sinatra

Goodnight, Sweetheart, Goodnight — The McGuire Sisters

The Heat's On — Rita Hayworth & Jose Ferrer

Here — Tony Martin

Hernando's Hideaway — Archie Bleyer

Hey There — Rosemary Clooney

The High And The Mighty — Les Baxter & His Orchestra

Hit And Run Affair — Perry Como

The Honeymoon's Over — Tennessee Ernie Ford & Betty Hutton

How Blue? — The Mills Brothers

I Can't Tell A Waltz From A Tango — Patti Page

I Could Have Told You — Frank Sinatra

I Really Don't Want To Know — Les Paul & Mary Ford

I Speak To The Stars — Doris Day

If I Give My Heart To You — Doris Day

If You Love Me (Really Love Me) — Kay Starr

I'm A Fool To Care — Les Paul & Mary Ford

In The Chapel In The Moonlight — Kitty Kallen

Indiscretion — Jo Stafford

It Happens To Be Me — Nat King Cole

It Worries Me — Frank Sinatra

It's A Woman's World — The Four Aces

Jilted — Teresa Brewer

The Little Shoemaker — The Gaylords

Little Things Mean A Lot — Kitty Kallen

The Lonesome Polecat — The McGuire Sisters

Love I You (You I Love) — The Gaylords

Lovin' Spree — Eartha Kitt

The Magic Tango — Hugo Winterhalter

Make Her Mine — Nat King Cole

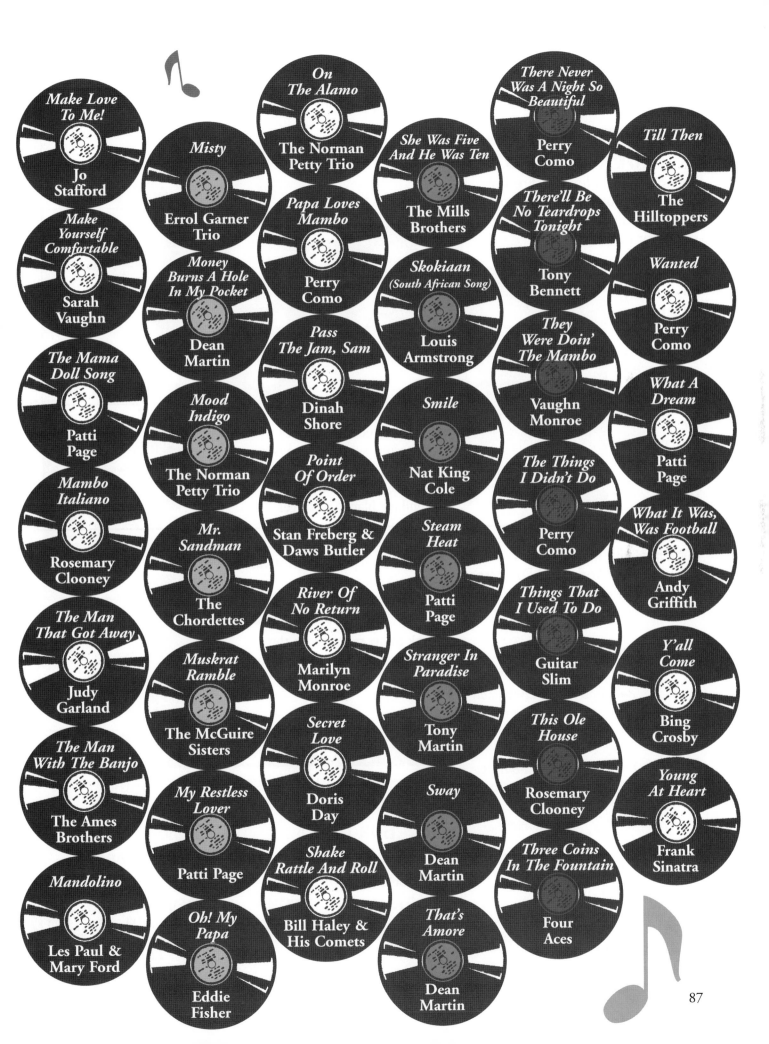

87

1954

GIVE 'EM THAT OLD ROCK 'N' ROLL

Young white audiences, tired of boring pop tunes, are turning to black radio stations and record stores for music.

Alan Freed

In Newark, New Jersey, DJ **Alan Freed's** first rock 'n' roll dance features the **Clovers,** the **Harptones** and **Muddy Waters**.

Alan Freed picks up a wider audience with his move to WINS Radio in New York, and DJs across America are encouraged to emulate his programming.

GONNA GET THOSE RIDIN' IN THE ELEVATOR BLUES

MUZAK develops a self-contained music operating system for industrial use.

PHILCO manufactures the first phonograph without a radio and Motorola produces the first high-fidelity record players.

• PASSING •

Raymond Hubbell, 75
One of the founders of ASCAP, Hubbell composed for Broadway musicals, including *Ziegfeld Follies*.

Billed as the "The Nation's Rockingest Rhythm Group," 29-year-old former DJ **BILL HALEY AND THE COMETS** record *(We're Gonna) Rock Around the Clock*.

Folkways Records releases a four-record set of 94 songs including *Jailhouse Blues* and *On Top of Old Smokey* by legendary black folksinger **Leadbelly**.

Leadbelly

The first Newport Jazz Festival is held in Rhode Island.

BLUE SKIES FOR SNOW

Hank Snow remains on the country-and-western charts for 52 weeks.

Hank Snow

FAMOUS BIRTHS

ADAM ANT
ELVIS COSTELLO
BOB GELDOF
DAVID HIDALGO
BRUCE HORNSBY
JERMAINE JACKSON
RICKIE LEE JONES
ANNIE LENNOX

PAT METHENY
CESAR ROSAS
DAVID LEE ROTH
RICKY SKAGGS
STEVIE RAY VAUGHAN
STEVE WARINER
NANCY WILSON
YANNI

WHAT A YEAR IT WAS!

You've never really enjoyed your records before
...nor had such a wonderful way to play them

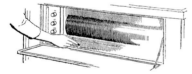

200 Selections at your finger tips

That's right! 200 selections, 100 records, of your favorite 45 r.p.m. music ready to play, instantly, automatically! . . . any or all . . . at the touch of a finger. With this wonderful instrument you may ar-

range programs to play one record . . . five records . . . or for as long as 25 hours without repetition. And all without touching a record . . . without handling an album. Once you see it, you'll agree the Select-O-Matic is the most remarkable development for playing recorded music since the invention of the phonograph.

Music that has new Tonal Realism

Once the program's arranged, just sit back and enjoy the music you never knew was on the records. Music that takes on added dimension and presence . . . music that has new tonal realism.

Music for your business?

Here's the practical, inexpensive method of bringing the acknowledged advantages of music to your business. Why not investigate?

Write. A descriptive folder and the name of your Seeburg Dealer will be sent on request.

J. P. SEEBURG CORPORATION
Chicago 22, Illinois

dependable music systems since 1902.

NO WORK . . . ALL PLAY . . . Seeburg Select-o-matic **200** MUSIC SYSTEMS

The Library Unit. Plays through TV, radio or other sound system. High fidelity pre-amplifier. Spring tension magnetic pickup with genuine diamond styluses. Limed oak cabinet.

The Custom Unit. For built-in music systems. Mounted on sturdy, double sliding metal track. High fidelity pre-amplifier. Spring tension magnetic pickup with genuine diamond styluses.

TRUE HIGH FIDELITY GIVES NEW TONAL REALISM

The Console. High fidelity power amplifier (20 watt — 20 to 30,000 cps range), high fidelity pre-amplifier, high fidelity dual coaxial speaker. Spring tension magnetic pickup, with genuine diamond styluses. Light Korina or rich mahogany wood cabinet.

New Compositions

The Odyssey of a Race
Heitor Villa-Lobos

~

Symphonie
André Jolivet

~

**Serenade for
Violin, Strings
and Percussion**
Leonard Bernstein

*Leonard
Bernstein*

~

Practical Cats
Alan Rawsthorne

~

Fourth Symphony
William Wordsworth

~

Ralph Vaughan Williams:
**Concerto for Bass Tuba
Hodie (This Day)
Violin Sonata in A Minor**

~

Igor Stravinsky:
**In Memoriam Dylan Thomas
Four Russian Peasant Songs**

Igor Stravinsky

Tenth Symphony
Dmitri Shostakovich
(American Premiere)

~

Symphonic Fantasy
Roy Harris

~

Concerto No. 5
Alan Hovhaness

~

**Concerto for Violin
and Orchestra**
Ernst Krenek

~

Dawn in a Tropical Forest
Heitor Villa-Lobos

*Heitor
Villa-Lobos*

~

Louisville Concerto
Jacques Ibert

~

Toccata Giocosa
Gardner Read

~

Second Symphony
Leroy Robertson

Classical music
represents 40% of
record sales this year.

87-year-old **Arturo
Toscanini** resigns as
conductor of the NBC
Symphony Orchestra,
ending a 68-year career.

AND ON A LIGHT NOTE

Comedian **Danny Kaye** is
guest conductor during a
special concert by the
Philadelphia Orchestra.

WHAT A YEAR IT WAS!

Opera News

Premieres

David
Darius Milhaud

Nelson
Lennox Berkeley

Gian Carlo Menotti

Moses and Aaron
Arnold Schoenberg
(unfinished work)

The Saint of Bleecker Street
Gian Carlo Menotti

Troilus and Cressida
William Walton

The Tender Land
Aaron Copland

The Turn of the Screw
Benjamin Britten

The Transposed Heads
Peggy Glanville-Hicks

Benjamin Britten

Marian Anderson

Marian Anderson becomes the first black singer to sign a contract with the Metropolitan Opera.

Peruvian multi-octaved **Yma Sumac** receives rave reviews following her concert in Carnegie Hall.

Maria Meneghini Callas makes her American debut at the Chicago Civic Opera House in *Norma*.

On a spring tour, the New York City Opera Company brings 81 performances of opera to 22 cities outside of New York.

Maria Callas

PULITZER PRIZE FOR MUSIC

Quincy Porter

Concerto Concertante for Two Pianos and Orchestra

WHAT A YEAR IT WAS!

1954

Dance

The Japanese **Azuma Kabuki Dancers** and **Musicians** tour the U.S.

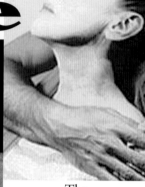

The **Martha Graham Company** dances at Italy's Florence Festival.

In her London debut, **Martha Graham** produces *Ardent Song* with music by **Alan Hovhaness**.

The New York City Ballet completes its European tour.

With choreography by **George Balanchine**, the New York City Ballet introduces a new version of **Peter I. Tchaikovsky's** THE NUTCRACKER.

George Balanchine choreographs WESTERN SYMPHONY, music by **Hershy Kay**, and IVESIANA, music by **Charles Ives**.

Roland Petit's Ballets de Paris performs in New York starring **Leslie Caron**, **Colette Marchand** and **Violette Verdy**.

Merce Cunningham is awarded a Guggenheim fellowship for choreography.

With **Moira Shearer** as guest artist, the Festival Ballet performs in Monte Carlo.

The Celtic Ballet of Scotland makes its first American appearance at the Jacob's Pillow Dance Festival.

JOSÉ LIMÓN choreographs *The Traitor* and DORIS HUMPHREY choreographs *Felipe el Loco* at the seventh American Dance Festival in New London, Connecticut.

Back in England after an American tour, the Sadler's Wells Ballet produces a new version of *Coppélia*, featuring MARGOT FONTEYN as one of the principal dancers.

Following the resignation of DAME ADELINE GENÉE, MARGOT FONTEYN is appointed president of the Royal Academy of Dancing.

LEONIDE MASSINE produces and dances in his *Le Tricorne* at the Rome Opera.

At La Scala, JEROME ROBBINS choreographs *Appalachian Spring* and *Mario and the Magician*.

JOSÉ LIMÓN and PAULINE KONER perform in the American Dance Festival at Connecticut College, New London, Connecticut.

Dancing to the music of DUKE ELLINGTON, the Rotterdam Ballet Ensemble produces *The Headless Hawk* and *Othello*, choreographed by LEO KERSLEY with music by GABRIEL FAURÉ.

MOST POPULAR BALLROOM DANCES WORLDWIDE

1. Fox Trot
2. Mambo
3. Tango
4. Waltz

No new dance crazes start this year and there are no outstanding dance scenes in theatre or film.

WHAT A YEAR IT WAS!

ON BROADWAY

BOB FOSSE DOES THE CHOREOGRAPHY FOR HIS FIRST BROADWAY SHOW, "THE PAJAMA GAME."

JULIE ANDREWS MAKES HER BROADWAY DEBUT AS POLLY IN SANDY WILSON'S "THE BOY FRIEND," SET IN THE 1920s.

John Raitt
and
Carol Haney
in
The Pajama Game

ANOTHER OPENING, ANOTHER NIGHT

ABIE'S
IRISH ROSE
(REVIVAL)

✳

ANNIVERSARY
WALTZ

✳

A MIDSUMMER
NIGHT'S DREAM
(REVIVAL)

✳

ALL SUMMER
LONG

✳

ANASTASIA

✳

THE BAD
SEED

Nancy Kelly and **Patty McCormack**
in *The Bad Seed*

WHAT A YEAR IT WAS!

Walter Matthau and **Cedric Hardwicke** in *The Burning Glass*

Maria Karnilova and **Peter Gennaro** in *By The Beautiful Sea*

THE BOY FRIEND
✵
THE BURNING GLASS
✵
BY THE
BEAUTIFUL SEA
✵
THE CAINE MUTINY
COURT~MARTIAL

OPENINGS

THE CONFIDENTIAL CLERK

✣

DEAR CHARLES

✣

FANNY

✣

FRAGILE FOX

✣

THE GIRL IN PINK TIGHTS

✣

THE GOLDEN APPLE

✣

HIS AND HERS

✣

HOME IS THE HERO

✣

THE IMMORALIST

✣

KING OF HEARTS

Ina Claire (standing), **Joan Greenwood** and **Claude Rains** in *The Confidential Clerk*

COULD BE TOO HOT TO HANDLE

Tennessee Williams completes *Cat on a Hot Tin Roof* and *Orpheus Descending*.

BARD IN THE PARK

Joseph Papp creates the New York Shakespeare Festival.

Christopher Plummer makes his Broadway debut as George Phillips in *The Starcross Story*, starring **Katherine Cornell**.

Hal Holbrook performs his one-man show, *Mark Twain Tonight!*

Victor Borge's one-man Broadway hit, *Comedy in Music*, begins its second year.

Victor Borge

MADEMOISELLE COLOMBE

✣

ONDINE

✣

THE PAJAMA GAME

✣

PETER PAN

✣

PORTRAIT OF A LADY

✣

QUADRILLE

✣

THE RAINMAKER

✣

THE TENDER TRAP

✣

THE THREE PENNY OPERA

✣

THE TRAVELING LADY

✣

UNDER MILKWOOD

WHAT A YEAR IT WAS!

WHERE *Pride* IS A DIVIDEND !

It has been said, in song and in verse, that the best things in life are free.

And we must say that we side with this romantic conjecture in at least one small regard. For we know that the finest reward of Cadillac ownership costs you nothing.

We have reference, quite naturally, to that wonderful feeling of pride that comes inevitably to new owners of new Cadillacs. It is, in the truest sense of the word, a dividend for your wisdom in choosing the "car of cars."

Of course, when a motorist takes title to his Cadillac, he *expects* to find great pride in his new possession. But we doubt if ever he is fully prepared for the heart-lifting moments which await him behind the wheel.

There is, for instance, the unforgettable memory of his first journey home . . . and of the joyous welcome of family and friends.

There is his unending pride and joy in the car's great beauty and performance and mechanical perfection.

There is his deep-felt satisfaction at seeing his family surrounded with Cadillac's great comfort and safety and luxury.

And there is his keen awareness of membership in the world's most distinguished fraternity of new car owners.

Won't you come in soon and let us give you a demonstration "preview" of these remarkable "Cadillac dividends"?

We know you would find it the most enlightening experience of your motoring life— and, for our own part, it would be a pleasure to introduce you to the Standard of the World.

Cadillac

YOUR CADILLAC DEALER

1954

From left, **John Williams**, **Gusti Huber** and **Maurice Evans** in *Dial "M" For Murder*

THE PIANO TODAY, THE STAGE TOMORROW

Harry Truman's daughter, **Margaret**, makes her dramatic debut in *Autumn Crocus* at a summer stock theater in Pennsylvania followed by 30-year-old socialite-heiress **Gloria Vanderbilt Stokowski**.

Terence Rattigan's play *Separate Tables*, consisting of two one-acts, *Table by the Window* and *Table Number Seven*, opens at London's St. James Theatre starring **Eric Portman**.

GONNA WASH THIS SHOW RIGHT OUT OF THEIR HAIR

After nearly five years and 1,925 performances of *South Pacific*, **Richard Rodgers** and **Oscar Hammerstein II** attend the closing night party.

SHE MIGHT GET A LITTLE HOT UNDER THE COLLAR

Ingrid Bergman is in London to play the title role in *Joan of Arc at the Stake*.

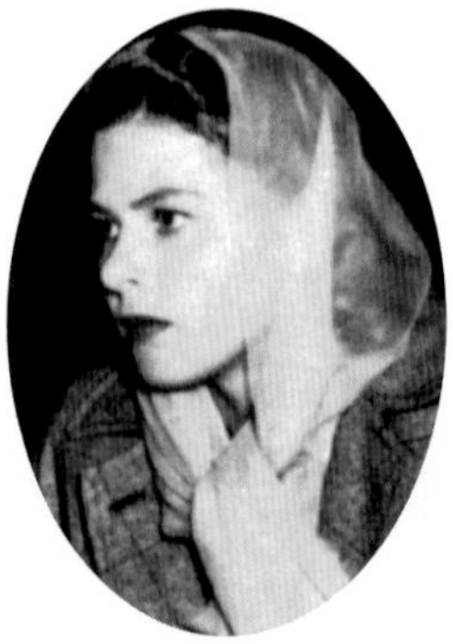

Another Closing, Another Night

All Summer Long

By The Beautiful Sea

Dial "M" For Murder

The Girl In Pink Tights

The King And I

My Three Angels

On Your Toes

Picnic

Portrait Of A Lady

South Pacific

The Traveling Lady

Wonderful Town

The World of Sholom Aleichem

TONY AWARDS 1954

PLAY
"The Teahouse Of The August Moon"
John Patrick (playwright)

MUSICAL PLAY
"Kismet"

DRAMATIC ACTOR
David Wayne
"The Teahouse Of The August Moon"

DRAMATIC ACTRESS
Audrey Hepburn
"Ondine"

MUSICAL ACTOR
Alfred Drake
"Kismet"

MUSICAL ACTRESS
Dolores Gray
"Carnival In Flanders"

DIRECTOR
Alfred Lunt
"Ondine"

CHOREOGRAPHER
Michael Kidd
"Can-Can"

Eartha Kitt gets good reviews in *Mrs. Patterson*, her first dramatic role in the U.S., which opens in Detroit for its pre-Broadway run.

PULITZER PRIZE FOR DRAMA
"THE TEAHOUSE OF THE AUGUST MOON"
John Patrick

NEW YORK DRAMA CRITICS' CIRCLE AWARDS

BEST PLAY
"THE TEAHOUSE OF THE AUGUST MOON"
John Patrick

BEST FOREIGN PLAY
"ONDINE"

BEST MUSICAL
"THE GOLDEN APPLE"

Famous Birth

—— **Harvey Fierstein** —

WHAT A YEAR IT WAS!

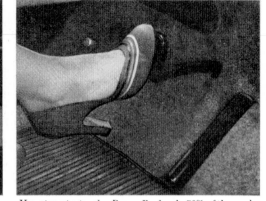

Silhouette-lighted instrument panel is a glare-free, glamorous complement to decorator-matched interiors. *You stop at a touch—Power Brakes do 50% of the work.*

From the moment you turn the key in a

DE SOTO AUTOMATIC

you do **less** and the **car** does **more**!

▶ **because of fully automatic no-clutch PowerFlite drive**

▶ **because of Full Time Power Steering and Power Brakes**

▶ **because of new engine might...new level ride...new balanced weight**

For instance, astonishingly smooth PowerFlite drive eliminates clutch and gearshift. Full Time Power Steering does 80% of your wheel work. Power Brakes cut your pedal effort in half. ▶ But these optional features are only part of the story. *No other car in its class matches De Soto's comfort features!* That road-hugging ride stems from a new full-width frame that's heavier than ever—plus No Sway Ride Control for sharp curves and corners. Five kinds of insulation cloak you in soothing silence. The lightning-bolt getaway is from Fire Dome's mighty 170 h.p. The rich, new interiors have the luxury of choice fabrics in beautiful weaves and textures. ▶ In *every* way that counts for driving that's better than ever—De Soto is the car of the year! Try a Fire Dome V-8 or Powermaster Six before *you* decide. ▶ De Soto Division, Chrysler Corporation.

DE SOTO-PLYMOUTH Dealers present **GROUCHO MARX** in "You Bet Your Life" every week on both RADIO and TELEVISION...NBC networks.

a new york
state of mind

ART

The **Whitney Museum's** annual assemblage of American art includes some greatly admired names in the art world, including **Robert Motherwell**, **Mark Tobey**, **Willem de Kooning**, **Jackson Pollock** and **Larry Rivers**.

The **Whitney Museum** leaves its Greenwich Village roots for more spacious uptown quarters.

Robert Motherwell

The refurbished **Metropolitan Museum of Art** opens 34 new galleries of mostly European decorative arts, displaying new acquisitions as well as many items not seen since World War II.

The **Guggenheim Museum** acquires its first **Cézanne**, "The Clock Maker."

The **Museum of Modern Art** turns 25. Included in its 400-piece anniversary retrospective are **Matisse's** "Piano Lesson" and **Picasso's** "Three Musicians" as well as works by **Pollock, Dali, Miro, Rouault, Hopper, van Gogh, Gauguin, de Kooning** and **Seurat**. **Nelson Rockefeller** donates "The Dream" by **Henri Rousseau**.

The **American Museum of Natural History** provides museum-goers with "guide-a-phone" technology, allowing them to take their own guided visit through the museum.

Robert Rauschenberg and **Jasper Johns** create window dressings for Tiffany's and Bonwit Teller in Manhattan.

Jasper Johns starts working on a painting of the American flag.

Robert Rauschenberg begins to create "combines," which combine elements of sculpture and painting into a single piece of art.

Jasper Johns

Self-portrait woodcut by Max Beckmann

In a fitting tribute to gallery owner **Curt Valentin**, his New York gallery mounts a memorial show featuring works by **Renoir, Klee, Beckmann, Gris, Degas, Calder, Arp, Rodin, Moore** and **Picasso**. Paintings and sculptures originally purchased from the gallery are borrowed from museums all over the country. Valentin's love of graphic arts and sculpture helped these art forms gain acceptance in America.

New York's Wildenstein Gallery mounts a Tibetan exhibit, with original Buddhist thankas, paintings and mandalas.

The Art Directors Club of New York puts on its 33rd advertising art show. Winners include **Irving Penn** for Gourielli perfume, **Richard Avedon** for a HARPER'S BAZAAR photo spread and **Andy Warhol** for the cover of INTERIORS magazine.

LOS ANGELES NEWS

Los Angeles' Municipal Art Center *(above)*, designed by **Frank Lloyd Wright**, is completed. The first exhibit is a display of Wright's creations, "Sixty Years of Living Architecture."

In Malibu, California, the **J. Paul Getty Museum** opens featuring ancient Greek and Roman art and beautiful gardens as well as tapestries, furniture and paintings from the 16th through 18th centuries.

Richard Diebenkorn paintings and drawings are on view at the **Paul Kantor Gallery**.

Celebrating the 300th anniversary of America's first Jewish settlement, a traveling show of American Jewish modern art is seen across the country. Participating artists include Max Weber, Jack Levine and Ben Shahn.

CHICAGO

Chicago's Arts Club exhibits **Picasso's** never-before-seen "Plaster Arm" and **Modigliani's** never-before-seen-in-America "Portrait of Madame Zborowski."

PENNSYLVANIA

The Pennsylvania Academy of the Fine Arts celebrates the 149th anniversary of the school and the 143rd anniversary of its annual exhibition. **John Marin** wins the Gold Medal for "Jersey Hills."

New galleries containing the $2 million **Louise and Walter Arensberg** collection open at the Philadelphia Museum of Art, with many pieces from modern art's beginnings. **Matisse, Braque, Miro, Brancusi, Klee, Picasso, Gris** and **Duchamp** are some of the well-known names that make up the vast collection.

Marcel Duchamp

WHAT A YEAR IT WAS!

ITALY

Leonardo da Vinci's self-portrait

BARGAIN BASEMENT PRICES FOR ITALIAN PAINTERS

A "Madonna and Child" sells for $450. The lucky owner is Hanna Teichert, who buys the painting in a New York antique store. After cleaning the painting, experts come to the conclusion that it is, indeed, a work by **Leonardo da Vinci.**

An estimated $80,000 **Botticelli** is found "for peanuts" by the Cincinnati Art Museum's Philip Adams while visiting Florence, Italy. The picture is a miniature version of Botticelli's "Judith."

A HORSE IS A HORSE, OF COURSE, UNLESS . . .

After much deliberation and high-tech testing, a horse in a Rome chapel fresco is proven to be a **Michelangelo.**

VENICE BIENNALE

Artists shown at the 27th Venice Biennale include **Arp, Bacon, Courbet, Dali, de Kooning, Ernst, Klee, Magritte, Picasso** and **Tanguy.**

VENICE BIENNALE WINNERS

Painting
Max Ernst   "The River Rhine"

Sculpture
Jean Arp   "Cobra Centaur"

Graphics
Joan Miro   Untitled

Passings

FRIDA KAHLO, 47

Married to artist Diego Rivera, the Mexican painter suffered physically throughout much of her life, which greatly influenced her paintings. Her work was widely shown in Europe and America, but there was only one exhibit in Mexico before her death. Her last diary entry said, "I hope the leaving is joyful and I hope never to return."

HENRI MATISSE, 84

Leader of the famed "Fauves," Matisse was one of a handful of painters in Paris at the turn of the century to break with convention and use color in a new and bold way. His extraordinary talent manifested itself in paintings, drawings, stained glass, ceramics, sculpture, textiles and other media. His many images of dancers are popular the world over.

This Year's Paintings

Marc Chagall	The Red Roofs
Salvador Dali	Crucifixion
Elaine de Kooning	Peter
Jean Dubuffet	Les Vagabonds
Max Ernst	Lonely
Fernand Léger	Acrobat And Horse
Pablo Picasso	Sylvette
Jackson Pollock	White Light
Graham Sutherland	Portrait Of Churchill

INTERNATIONAL AUCTION HIGHLIGHTS

Pierre-Auguste Renoir	*Young Girl Combing Her Hair*	$44,000
Claude Monet	*Peonies* (highest price for a Monet at auction)	$30,050
Camille Pissarro	*Garden of a House at Berneval*	$17,000
Grant Wood	*Daughters of the American Revolution* (charcoal sketch)	$2,800

A Chippendale bookcase goes for $17,300, while a bejeweled snuffbox that once belonged to Frederick the Great, and more recently Egypt's deposed King Farouk, sells at Sotheby's for $43,060.

FOR SALE

Andy Warhol paintings & drawings	$25-$100
Winslow Homer paintings	$1,200
Piet Mondrian charcoal	$10,000
Fernand Léger ceramics	$400-$1,500

JUST A FEW ODDS & ENDS

Picasso's "The Crane" sculpture, seen in a London show and comprised of forks, a shovel and other household items, is available for $6,000.

Merry Old England

The City Council of Manchester, England votes against buying Henry Moore's "Draped Torso." Discussions ensue as to whether or not the sculpture is art. It can be seen, along with other Moore bronzes, at London's Leicester Galleries.

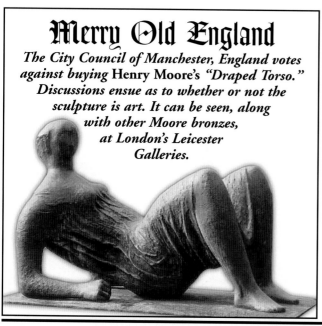

do-it-yourself...

it takes 3 steps to install a new

Webcor Diskchanger

If your present radio-phonograph combination is more than 5 years old, it is probably robbing you of the enjoyment of the magnificent new musical recordings on 33⅓ and 45 rpm records.

It will take you about an hour—and three easy-to-follow steps to completely modernize your present set with a world-famous, high-fidelity Webcor 3-speed automatic Diskchanger. From $49.50*

1 Visit your local radio, music or department store. Your dealer will tell you which model will fit into the space you have.

2 Remove the old player according to simple directions in Webcor's Do-It-Yourself Booklet.

3 Install your new, three-speed automatic Webcor according to easy-to-follow directions. It takes about an hour for the average home music enthusiast.

See your Webcor dealer today; your free copy of the simple installation booklet is waiting for you. If your dealer's supply has been exhausted, write to Customer Service Department, Webcor, Chicago 39.

all music sounds better on a

WEBCOR

Slightly higher West and subject to change without notice. © W/C 1954 **Chicago 39, Illinois**

Books 1954

Nobel Prize for Literature

Ernest Hemingway, USA

"For his mastery of the art of narrative, most recently demonstrated in *The Old Man and the Sea*, and for the influence that he has exerted on contemporary style."

Pulitzer Prizes

HISTORY
A Stillness At Appomattox
Bruce Catton

BIOGRAPHY OR AUTOBIOGRAPHY
The Spirit Of St. Louis
Charles A. Lindbergh

POETRY
The Waking
Theodore Roethke

NATIONAL REPORTING
Richard Wilson
Des Moines Register & Tribune

INTERNATIONAL REPORTING
Jim G. Lucas
Scripps-Howard Newspapers

EDITORIAL CARTOONING
Herbert L. Block
Washington Post & Times-Herald

American Academy of Arts & Letters

AWARD OF MERIT
Ernest Hemingway

Caldecott Award
(Children's Picture Book)

Madeline's Rescue
Ludwig Bemelmans

Senator John F. Kennedy begins his second book, *Profiles in Courage*.

Dr. John D. Kershaw of Colchester, England finds fault with the children's story *Cinderella* because he feels it doesn't prepare girls for the reality and challenges of marriage.

Kennedy

Septuagenarian American poets **Carl Sandburg** and **Robert Frost** receive awards from the Limited Editions Club for having bodies of work that seem destined to live on as classics. **Ernest Hemingway, John Steinbeck, William Faulkner, Rachel Carson** and **H.L. Mencken** are also honored.

Frost

Simone de Beauvoir is awarded France's Goncourt Prize for *Les mandarins*. It is the country's most prestigious literary award.

Someone finally returns *David Crockett: His Life and Adventures* to the Toledo, Ohio library. The book was due back in 1882.

DUMB & DUMBER
During a lecture in Chicago, **John Dos Passos** laments the current deficiency of the American public in "understanding of the English language."

SAY IT AIN'T SO, SUPERMAN
Dr. Fredric Wertham publishes *Seduction of the Innocent*, an attack on the comic book industry.

The American Library Association confers its Letter award on the Boston Public Library for "its courageous and continuing defense of freedom of inquiry and freedom to read."

Poet **W.H. Auden** is elected to the American Academy of Arts & Letters.

EVERYONE'S A CRITIC
Beverly Hills, California postal inspectors find what they consider obscene material addressed to a bookstore. *Lysistrata*, by Greek playwright Aristophanes, was written approximately 410 B.C. and is the tale of Athenian women who withhold sexual favors from their husbands until they stop waging war.

Lysistrata haranguing the Athenian women. Aubrey Beardsley illustration.

Passings

Colette, 81
One of the great French writers of the 20th century, Colette wrote dozens of novels and even more short stories. She was the first woman member and president of the Académie Goncourt and a grand officer of the French Legion of Honor. She used her own experiences in her prose and chose a virtually unknown Audrey Hepburn to star in *Gigi* on Broadway.

James Hilton, 54
Writer of such timeless classics as *Goodbye, Mr. Chips* and *Lost Horizon*, which both became successful motion pictures.

105

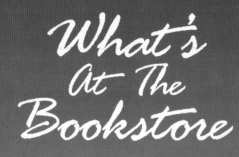

What's At The Bookstore

The Alice B. Toklas Cook Book
Alice B. Toklas

•

An Almanac Of Liberty
William O. Douglas

•

Atoms In The Family
Laura Fermi

•

The Bad Seed
William March

•

The Benchley Roundup
edited by Nathaniel Benchley

•

Benton's Row
Frank Yerby

•

The Bird's Nest
Shirley Jackson

•

Black Power
Richard Wright

•

The Blackboard Jungle
Evan Hunter

The Bridge Over The River Kwai
Pierre Boulle

•

The Bright Sands
Robert Lewis Taylor

•

A Child's Christmas In Wales
Dylan Thomas
(posthumously)

•

Collected Poems, 1923-1953
Louise Bogan

•

The Collected Poems Of Wallace Stevens

•

Confessions Of Felix Krull, Confidence Man
Thomas Mann

•

Cress Delahanty
Jessamyn West

•

The Desert Music And Other Poems
William Carlos Williams

•

The Dollmaker
Harriette Arnow

•

The Doors Of Perception
Aldous Huxley

W. Somerset Maugham

The Egyptian
Mika Waltari

•

A Fable
William Faulkner

•

The Fellowship Of The Ring
J.R.R. Tolkien

•

The Floating World
James A. Michener

•

Future Indefinite
Noel Coward

•

Have Tux Will Travel: Bob Hope's Own Story As Told To Peter Martin

•

Huge Season
Wright Morris

•

The Invisible Writing
Arthur Koestler

•

Let's Eat Right To Keep Fit
Adelle Davis

Louis Armstrong

Life With Groucho
Arthur Marx

•

Live And Let Die
Ian Fleming

•

Lord Of The Flies
William Golding

•

Love Is Eternal
Irving Stone

•

Mary Anne
Daphne du Maurier

•

Mine The Harvest
Edna St. Vincent Millay
(posthumously)

•

**Most Likely
To Succeed**
John Dos Passos

•

**Mr. Maugham
Himself**
W. Somerset Maugham

**My Several
Worlds: A
Personal Record**
Pearl S. Buck

•

**Never Victorious,
Never Defeated**
Taylor Caldwell

•

The Nightmare
C.S. Forester

•

**No Time For
Sergeants**
Mac Hyman

•

Not As A Stranger
Morton Thompson

•

**Poems
1923-1954**
e e Cummings

•

The Ponder Heart
Eudora Welty

•

**Quite Early
One Morning**
Dylan Thomas
(posthumously)

•

**R.S.V.P.:
Elsa Maxwell's
Own Story**
Elsa Maxwell

The Rebel
Albert Camus

•

The Royal Box
Frances Parkinson Keyes

•

**Satchmo: My Life
In New Orleans**
Louis Armstrong

•

Sayonara
James Michener

**The Second Tree
From The Corner**
E.B. White

•

**A Spy In The
House Of Love**
Anais Nin

•

**Survival Through
Design**
Richard J. Neutra

•

Sweet Thursday
John Steinbeck

•

**The View From
Pompey's Head**
Hamilton Basso

FASHION 1954

Sportswear guru Claire McCardell brings out her fall line, which, for the first time, includes accessories.

Her jersey evening dress is accessorized with a chunky necklace and large earrings.

A fleece suit is finished off with yellow gloves and yellow sunglasses.

A thick red turtleneck sweater tops a leather skirt.

Matching red socks reach almost to the knee.

Patterned pants are topped by a solid tank top. Flat shoes and a thick bracelet, along with a colorful necklace and matching earrings, complete the look.

Getting into the SWIM of Things

These gals are talking about the latest fashion in swimming attire, a suit with a built-in girdle.

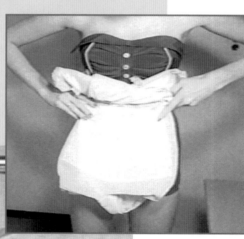

All set for an afternoon of play on Long Island Sound at Mamaroneck, New York. Judy, Florence and June, looking lovely in their stylish new suits by SURF DOGS, are looking forward to an afternoon of fun.

June and Dorothy play a game of Scrabble to while away the afternoon.

Judy is wearing a "Bloomer Girl" number with shirred hips (*left*), while in June's suit the accent is on the winged bra.

June dons a broad-brimmed straw hat and sunglasses to keep the sun out of her eyes as Judy poses on the seawall in her schoolgirl romper suit.

Have a great summer, girls!

WHITE WALL WHITE...

...the clean, bright color that picks up
and points out every beautiful detail of
Ship'n Shore's soft-tailored
broadcloth blouses. 2⁹⁸

Ship'n Shore®

BLOUSES

The styles shown,
sizes 30 to 40,
white or colors...
fine combed cotton
broadcloth, $2.98.
Others in silky-soft
Wamsutta pima
cotton, $3.98.
Child's blouse,
7 to 14...
$1.98.

Ship'n Shore®

112

FASHIONS FOR STARS ON HOLIDAY

1954

Just off the set of the film *Yankee Pasha is* blonde **Mamie Van Doren** *wearing a cotton print travel suit topped off by a handmade Italian straw pixie hat.*

Ruth Hampton *and* **Kathleen Hughes** *look lovely in their holiday fashions.*

Colleen Miller *is all set for happy holiday doings in her colorful new outfit, especially good for California wear.*

Lara Corday *shows up sporting a very slim pooch and a very nice tan, and she'll keep the tan in this black and gold cotton print halter dress.*

1954

Polka dots

are one of the most popular prints of the year and can be seen on dresses, gloves, blouses, handbags, sweaters and anything else in Madame's wardrobe.

For that special evening out, a strapless, sparkly, deep V décolletage, almost-to-the-floor dress by famed designer Pierre Balmain should set you apart from the crowd.

1954

YOU GO, COCO!

The #1 woman of french style, **Coco Chanel** returns to the fashion limelight and shows her first collection since retiring15 years ago.

Karl Lagerfeld begins his first job in fashion—working for **Pierre Balmain** in Paris.

Christian Dior introduces his "H" look, aimed at making any woman, even the curvy one, seem more slender and youthful. Signature designs for the look included dropped waistlines, flat silhouettes, narrow shoulders and slim bosoms. The new look has many opponents, including full-figured Marilyn Monroe.

Winter woolen coats are thick with extra-large buttons and cuffs, often topped with a wool hat.

THE PRESIDENT AND MAMIE EISENHOWER

are "among the most shoe-conscious folks ever to occupy the White House," according to the periodical *Leather and Shoes*.

JACQUES FATH brings out sheer stockings with patterns including polka dots and leopard prints.

IF THE SHOE FITS...

Roughly 500 million pairs of shoes are made in America.

A simulated pearl choker with matching drop earrings finish off any outfit for just a few dollars.

NEW YORK'S NEWEST
Fancy Manhattan shops sell earrings with glass fishbowls containing live guppies.

YO, BUDDY, VINI, VIDI, VICI

Designer **James Galanos** votes for Roman women as the world's best dressed in the evenings while New York gals are the tops during the day. As for women in California, Los Angeles-based Galanos feels, "The women are likely to be too casual in the daytime and overdressed at night."

The first Canadian fashion show held abroad brings dozens of reporters to New York's Hotel Pierre.

According to psychiatrist **Dr. Edmund Bergler** in his book, FASHION AND THE UNCONSCIOUS, male fashion designers unconsciously dislike women and aren't creating fashions to make women look beautiful, but to make them ill at ease.

1954

HAIR & MAKEUP

Influenced by **Alexander Calder**, Manhattan hairdresser **Victor Vito** cuts ladies' tresses to resemble the movement of mobiles.

Toni's first foray into cosmetics results in the smear-proof lipstick, "Viv."

A concealing stick called "Erace" is brought out by **Max Factor** to cover up dark circles under the eyes.

"WINNIE" WINNER
(COTY AMERICAN FASHION CRITICS AWARD)
James Galanos

NEIMAN-MARCUS AWARD
James Galanos
Emilio Pucci

PASSINGS

Jacques Fath, 42
One of the great French designers, Fath entered fashion after a career in banking. His flamboyance and showmanship was displayed in his clothes, fashion shows and parties. He loved designing haute couture, yet his ready-to-wear line was successful in some of America's top department stores.

Kokichi Mikimoto, 96
A one-time noodle entrepreneur, Mikimoto gained world fame for inventing a way to create cultured pearls.

little travelers love their

BAMBURY

Coats for girls WITH ADD-A-YEAR* HEMS

Coats designed for dress-up . . . for days when little girls need to look their loveliest. And Add-A-Year* Hems give them an extra season's wear.
left: Brown, grey, winter blue, American beauty, turquoise or plum poodle cloth. Genuine seal fur outlines the velvet collar. *right:* 100% wool fleece in red, nude, turquoise, honey, pink, cotillion, berry, copen or green. Bambury coats and coat-sets come in toddler to mid-teen sizes 1 to 14 from $20 to $45.

for the little lasses

For day — Dresses touch just above the knee with a bow, perhaps with a frilly blouse underneath. Mary Jane shoes with white socks adorn the feet.

For night — Cozy feety pajamas.

BELTS
WITH
BRASS BUCKLES

STRIPED
OR
PATTERNED
TIES

SINGLE-BREASTED
SUITS IN BROWN,
GRAY OR BLUE

Diplomat **Porfirio Rubirosa** and **President Eisenhower** are some of America's best-dressed men. A surprised Studebaker-Packard chairman of the board, **Paul Hoffman**, makes the cut as well, stating, "My family criticizes me for being a sloppy dresser."

President Eisenhower

1-2-3-4 WE WANT CLOTHES AND WE WANT MORE

Not necessarily known for its fashionable uniforms, the Army reveals an updated look for its enlisted folk, which includes black shoes, a green coat, a tan shirt and a brown tie.
Gone is the Eisenhower jacket.

OVERCOATS YEAR-ROUND

Five-year-old **Prince Charles** is voted the world's best-dressed man by *Tailor and Cutter* magazine.

Young Prince Charles

What a powerful difference this <u>high-octane</u> gasoline makes!

Ask any pilot. He'll tell you how important high-octane gasoline is to a plane's engine. Well, the same goes for today's automobile engines. You see, the octane rating of a gasoline determines how much power it can deliver. That's why it's so important to be sure you always get a *high-octane* fuel. And the easy way to be sure is to look for the familiar yellow-and-black "Ethyl" emblem on the pump. You'll find that "Ethyl" gasoline makes a powerful difference . . . every mile you drive!

ETHYL CORPORATION
New York 17, N. Y.
Ethyl Antiknock Ltd., in Canada

*Enjoy full power—
use high-octane
"ETHYL" gasoline!*

122

HAVE PIANO, WILL TRAVEL

A new portable, stringless, electronic piano is being offered by Miessner Inventions, Inc.

SKIING
FOR ALL SEASONS

A Connecticut inventor gets patent for snowmaking device.

A traveling sidewalk is installed between the Erie and H&M Jersey City railroad stations.

NO MORE FEET HANGING OVER THE EDGE

A new standard "king size" mattress geared for tall men is now available.

AH, THIS ONE IS JUST RIGHT

The "Score Master," a testing device designed to help amateur and professional golfers determine which ball is best for them, is being marketed by Eze Golf Corp.

POP IT IN THE OVEN AND IT'S DINNER

Swanson

frozen TV dinners hit ovens all over the country.

THEY'RE NOT JUST WHISTLING PEPPERONI

Edward Plummer and his partner, Sherwood "Shakey" Johnson, open SHAKEY'S Pizza Parlor in Sacramento.

FLIES NO MORE

Flies who get too close to the new "insect electrocuting appliance" will get the shock of their lives from this device, which traps and electrocutes them and gets rid of their remains.

ADD A LITTLE WATER AND PRESTO

Carnation brings you its new instant nonfat dry milk.

NUTS TO YOU

Mars adds all-brown peanut *M&Ms* to its candy line.

POP-UP PANCAKES

The **Quaker Oats Co.** is testing at the retail level prebaked, frozen pancakes that are heated up in a toaster.

Breads and cakes are now being baked in cans and vacuum-sealed at the oven, keeping the product fresh for months.

AND FOR ALL YOU TELEVISION FANS

Schlitz Brewing Co. is test-marketing in 26 states a new 16-ounce can of beer.

Already test-marketing its sparkling water, **Schweppes** adds ginger ale to its list of soft drinks.

A JUICY EXPERIENCE

Thanks to a new process that bombards fresh juice with ultraviolet rays, Florida orange juice is now available in waxed cartons in the refrigerator section of your market for 35¢ a quart.

The dairy industry will soon be coming out with new strawberry-flavored milk.

JUST POUR AND STIR

The U.S. Department of Agriculture adds powdered tomato juice to its list of fruit juice powders.

BUT WILL YOUR LIPS STILL PUCKER?

Sunkist Growers is testing frozen lemon juice.

WHAT A YEAR IT WAS!

SPEEDY WAY TO PEEL THOSE SPUDS

Hoffritz for Cutlery has a new automatic potato peeler that removes vegetable skin quickly and in one continuous stroke.

CHILL IN (OR OUT)

A new butter dish, the "Buttermaster," is available with a hermetically sealed refrigerant that keeps the butter cold while it's on the table.

A new ice cream mixer that fits into the freezer is being made available by **Auburn Button Works**.

SOON MOMS WILL BE OUT OF CHIPS

Researchers at the University of Illinois promise housewives that non-chip pots and pans are in their future thanks to a new titanium enamel with which researchers are experimenting.

THIS ONE'S FOR THE NUTS

The world's first electronic nutcracker, which explodes walnuts out of their shells, is being manufactured by **Northwest Nut Growers**.

YOU'RE TOAST

Proctor Electric has brought out an electric toaster that can toast a piece of bread in just one minute.

JAVA IN A JIFFY

New $30 automatic coffeemakers that brew two cups of coffee in four minutes are introduced in New York. Not to be outdone, **Westinghouse** launches a percolator capable of brewing nine cups of coffee in nine minutes.

NO MORE SLIP SLIDING AWAY

A new liquid rubber plastic called "Griptex" is developed for skid-proofing rugs.

Micro-Moisture Controls has developed the "Weathervane Venetian" window that causes the window to automatically close when it rains.

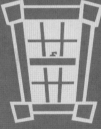

A TEASPOON FOR YOU AND A TEASPOON FOR YOUR FURNACE

General Electric research engineers discover that milk of magnesia is the best tonic for keeping furnace nuts and bolts from melting together.

A HELPFUL STICKY SITUATION

You can now line your shelves with adhesive-backed vinyl "Con-Tact" paper.

To make clothes softer, housewives can now add "Nu-Soft" to the final rinse water.

More than 120 lbs. of frozen food easily stored in the big freezer section *at the bottom* of this new kind of refrigerator.

"Up-Side-Down" refrigerator!

*Now—makers of famous Dual-Temp give you full family-size home
freezer and refrigerator—all in one. Never needs defrosting!*

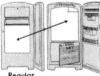

Regular   "Up-Side-Down"
9 cu. ft.

**UP TOP—more storage capacity than in regular
9 cu. ft. refrigerator.** Compare actual food-storage
space of this new kind of refrigerator with any
regular refrigerator. It's big! And it's all in easy-
reach position—no bending or stooping.

**AT THE BOTTOM—giant freezer holds 2¾ bushels
of frozen food.** Freezes food at 20° below zero—
coldest cold of any refrigerator-freezer. Just right
for *safe* quick freezing. Zero can be dialed for regular frozen food storage.

TWO TEMPERATURE CONTROLS—one for the Sub-Zero Freezer, one
for the Humid Cold Compartment • **TWO ROLL OUT SHELVES** —
easily cleaned, rust resistant • **ULTRA-VIOLET LAMP** in the humid-
cold compartment helps purify the air, retards growth of mold and
bacteria. See it at your Admiral Dealer's now.

Admiral Refrigerators start as low as $179.95

Admiral

Makers of the famous Dual-Temp

1954

NOW IF IT COULD ONLY BRING ME MY POTATO CHIPS

"Controla-Tone" is a new electronic volume-control gadget for television, radio or phonographs and can be operated from the comfort of your easy chair.

Complete with a high-pitched, tinny sound, the first pocket-size transistor radios hit the stores.

General Electric develops a small radio receiver that can be worn like a hearing aid.

LULLABY AND GOOD NIGHT

RCA introduces a clock-radio that can be preset with two different stations— one to go to sleep by and the other to wake up by.

The Cascade Mountains at Jim Creek Valley, Washington are the site of the world's most powerful radio transmitter now in operation.

Mohawk Business Machines is manufacturing a pocket-size, battery-operated tape recorder weighing 3 1/4 pounds that can record for up to an hour.

Bell Telephone Labs demonstrates a solar battery that converts rays of sun directly into electrical energy.

IBM unveils an all-transistor calculator requiring only 5% of the power of its electronic counterpart.

California's **Texas Instruments** brings out the first practical silicon transistor.

AND IT DOESN'T TAKE COFFEE BREAKS

An automatic secretary in the form of a telephone-answering device is developed by Bell Laboratories and is being distributed to telephone companies by **Western Electric**.

"Telehold" is a new device that snaps onto your telephone receiver allowing you to use your telephone hands-free.

I HEARD WHAT YOU SAID!!

The development of "Port-A-Phone," a new wireless intercom that plugs into any standard outlet, is announced by **General Industrial Company**.

YOU LIGHT UP MY DIAL

AT&T has announced the development of a new telephone handset that lights up when in use.

CORD-FREE HEARING AIDS

Hearing aid cords will be no longer be dangling out of your ears now that the **Maico Co.** has developed a new all-transistor hearing aid.

SEEING IS HEARING

A new hearing aid is available that comes embedded in the frame of horn-rimmed glasses.

NO MORE STATIC

Electricity-free hairbrushes manufactured with plastic backs and bristles hit the marketplace.

NOW IF WE COULD JUST USE IT ON THOSE HIPS

Max Factor introduces a new camouflage stick for blemishes and circles under the eyes.

A new electric clutch has been designed for farm equipment allowing the farmer to operate his machines continuously with repeated stops.

THIS IS NO ORDINARY SQUIRT

With a simple twist of the attachment's head, **Bete Fog Nozzle's** new garden hose squirts a straight stream of water almost twice as far as ordinary nozzles.

WEEDING OUT THE WEEDS THE EASY WAY

Porter-Cable introduces an electric grass trimmer for use in areas lawn mowers can't reach.

SEE... BIGGER ISN'T ALWAYS BETTER

Westinghouse develops the world's smallest lamp bulb measuring only 1/20th of an inch in diameter while **General Electric** revolutionizes the photography habits of the nation with its new "m-2," the world's smallest flashbulb, retailing for 10¢ apiece.

Minox Company develops a new tiny camera, so small that it can be carried in the pocket like a fountain pen or cigarette lighter.

According to experts, the new **Leica** 35mm camera is ushering in a new era in photographic convenience.

General Motors introduces the XP-21 Firebird, the first gas turbine-powered automobile.

THEY'RE TAKING THE WRAP

In order to reduce blind spots, Buicks, Cadillacs and Oldsmobiles are now equipped with wraparound windshields.

Hailed as the greatest innovation since tetraethyl lead introduced in the 1920s, U.S. oil companies launch premium-grade gas.

Manufacturing of reflective clothing begins with stocking caps.

Norco Manufacturing Co. creates a "black light" fluorescent ultraviolet pencil that is invisible on white or light surfaces but will fluoresce a brilliant green when activated by the pencil.

WHAT A YEAR IT WAS!

The Air Force School of Aviation Medicine in Randolph Field, Texas receives the "sealed cabin," the first piece of experimental equipment built specifically for the study of living conditions in space.

THE LIGHT, TOUGH WONDER METAL

The U.S. government has authorized the exploration of uses for titanium by civilian manufacturers.

IS THAT A FLY IN THE OINTMENT?

A new X-ray microscope that can look inside specimens has been developed by **General Electric** and is capable of wide use in medical science, biology and industry.

NO MORE COUNTING ON YOUR FINGERS?

Dr. B.F. Skinner, professor of psychology at Harvard University, has come up with a machine for teaching arithmetic.

BUT WILL IT CARRY THE GROCERIES TO MY CAR?

National Cash Register has developed a fast-thinking cash register that adds up your grocery bill and tells you how much change you have coming.

MOM CAN COOK WHILE BABY IS ROCKING

In the near future, mothers may be able to purchase a self-rocking baby carriage thanks to a portable rocker called "Rock a Bye" designed by Dr. Gordon H. Strom, professor and research engineer in N.Y.U.'s Guggenheim School of Aeronautics.

RAIN DANCERS NEED NOT APPLY

Dr. Paul B. MacCready Jr. invents a "robot cloud-seeding generator," or a rainmaking machine.

The **Warren Refining and Chemical Co.** has developed a fire-resistant paint.

Master Lock brings out a pick-proof padlock.

You can now get an instant tan with an overhead lamp fixture made by Travel Tan.

IF YOU CAN'T STAND THE HEAT, LET THE FAN TURN ITSELF ON

Westinghouse Electric has a new automatic timer for fans.

SHINE ON THE RUN

Now you can have a quick shoeshine with "Show Mitt," which contains wax on one side and a buffing cloth on the other.

PASSINGS

Jacques Brandenberger, 81 Inventor of cellophane.

Dr. William Lowell, 94 Inventor of the golf tee.

You're the "Lazy Susan" in this step-saver kitchen

Y OU'VE seen conventional Lazy Susans with their rotating shelves that put everything at your finger tips without making you reach or take a step. Here's something different—a kitchen that just reverses the idea—and makes *you* the Lazy Susan. You stand in the center of a comfortable counter "island" that has all the important kitchen appliances built in. Instead of walking from one part of the kitchen to another, you just turn around, and you're in front of the stove, sink, cutting block, or oven —whichever you need. Pass-through windows even make it possible to serve the dining room or terrace from the cooking island.

Besides the new switch on the Lazy Susan idea, this kitchen has something else you haven't seen before. It's the beautiful rainbow-hued floor of Armstrong's Royelle Linoleum,

a bold new styling of classic marble graining in rich modern colorings.

To make full use of its decorative value, the Royelle Linoleum has been coved up the base of the counters and almost all the way up the sides of the snack bar. This decorating trick helps to blend the work-center island into the rest of the room. It's a practical idea, too, since it does away with dirt-catching corners at the base of the counter and makes the front of the snack bar scuff-proof and easy to clean.

Armstrong's Royelle Linoleum is available in 14 beautiful color combinations. See them at your Armstrong merchant's store this week.

Slide-through shelves at the snack bar make it possible to set dishes and silver in place for the next meal as soon as they're washed and dried. Shelves and counter tops are Armstrong's new plastic Granette Corlon, white, No. 6107. The floor is Armstrong's Royelle Linoleum, No. 1513, a practical choice for any kitchen. Good looking and comfortable underfoot, it has a virtually seamless surface that requires little care. For a free floor plan of this kitchen and a list of furnishings, just send us a post card today.

Send for new decorating book, "It's Easy to Decorate" —36 full-color pages filled with exciting decorating ideas for every room in your house, old or new. Send 10¢ today (40¢ outside U.S.A.) to Armstrong Cork Co., 5403 Madison Street, Lancaster, Pa.

ARMSTRONG'S LINOLEUM

There's an Armstrong Floor for every room in your home

LINOLEUM ○ CORLON® ● LINOTILE® ● RUBBER TILE ● CORK TILE ● ASPHALT TILE ● EXCELON TILE ● VINOFLOR® ● QUAKER® RUGS AND FLOOR COVERINGS

The world's smallest jet, a delta-winged plane, is ready for flight in France.

Tiny Plane
TAKES FLIGHT

Weighing less than 1,400 pounds, it is 15 feet long and has a wing spread of 16 feet. Little it may be, but its performance figures are remarkable.

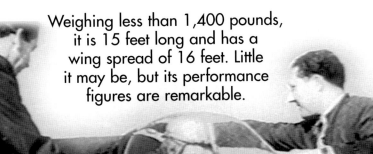

With a thrust of a mere 320 pounds, the tiny delta wing cruises at a whopping 320 mph.

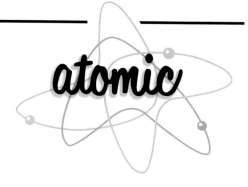

ARE WOMEN WINNING THE BATTLE OF THE SEXES?

In his new book entitled *Women: Man's Equal?* Sir Adolphe Abrahams contends that women are biologically superior to men, even though they have only 67% of man's muscular capacity, and have greater moral courage.

ANOTHER STRENGTH FOR THE "WEAKER SEX"

The Prudential Insurance Company reports that women withstand high blood pressure much better than men.

NOTHING THAT A LITTLE PAYCHECK WOULDN'T FIX

The humdrum, thankless and payless nature of daily housework may explain why more women suffer from headaches than men.

BETTER SHARPEN THOSE KILLING SKILLS

A Scotland Yard commander is quoted in the *Chicago Daily Tribune*, saying that women murderers are crueler than men in that many times they choose poison and watch their victims suffer for weeks whereas men generally kill quickly and mercifully.

Be It Ever So Humble

As families find more pleasure in staying home rather than going to movies or costly nightclubs, demand for products for the home is growing.

SEEING IS BELIEVING

In a report to the International Congress of Ophthalmology, it is revealed that atomic energy is being used for the treatment of eye cancer.

ALL WE NEED IS THE OLD LACE

Massachusetts General Hospital is using radioactive arsenic to locate brain tumors.

PASSING

Enrico Fermi, 53

Nobel Prize-winning, Italian-born physicist Fermi left Italy for the United States where he became a professor. As head of the government-sponsored Manhattan Project, Fermi worked with other scientists to develop an atomic bomb. He oversaw the creation of the world's first working nuclear reactor and produced the first nuclear chain reaction. With his discoveries, the atomic age was born.

New mountain chains are found in the Pacific Ocean, between Hawaii and the Marshall Islands, and in the Arctic Ocean, which appears to be divided into two basins.

"HOT" FASHIONS

From Hanford Plutonium Works, a look at the latest in fashions for atomic energy technicians working in hot areas.

This room is contaminated with radioactive dust, and that "plastic gargoyle" *(left)* is the newest type of safety suit with a long, hollow tail that allows the technician to enter from outside *(above)*.

The suit is kept inflated by a slightly higher air pressure than the hot room and the technician wears a face mask to ensure a fresh air supply. It's a great improvement over earlier safe coveralls—bulky, cumbersome and likely to accumulate contaminated dust. The new suit cuts out some really impressive laundry bills.

A transparent face piece gives clear vision.

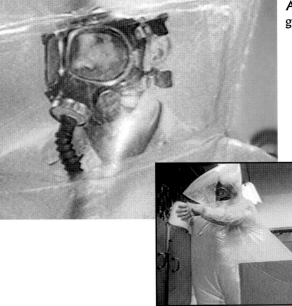

Shielded from hot particles by the plastic skin, the technician does his job in reasonable comfort.

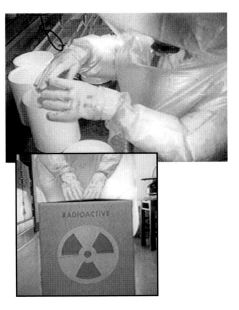

The suit looks weird but is practical.

Another example of the ingenuity that keeps our atomic plants safe.

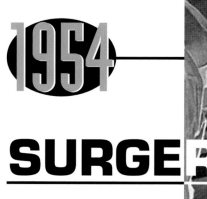

SURGERY

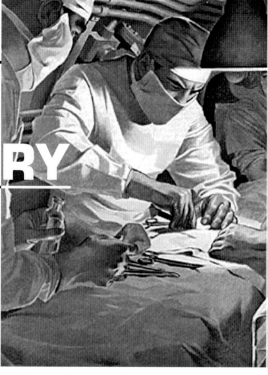

The *Archives of Surgery* reports on a new plastic dressing that can be sprayed on burns and surgical wounds.

ARE YOU TAPING THIS?

The medical journal *GP* reports the successful closing of 91 skin lacerations using cellophane tape instead of stitches.

DO YOU KNOW "MELANCHOLY BABY"?

A U.S. Air Force surgeon has begun using music piped in through earphones on surgical patients and says that the soothing and relaxing sound of music contributes to narcosis or deep sleep.

According to the director of the Sloan-Kettering Institute, cancer surgery has been made safer by the development of chemicals that control the clotting of blood.

GETTING OFF SHAKY GROUND

Dr. Irving S. Cooper of New York reports a new surgery for Parkinson's disease that could help relieve trembling.

BILL CUT THE MUSTARD

In Toronto, Dr. William Mustard performs the first successful heart surgery aided by hypothermia.

Richard Herrick receives the organ from his twin brother, Ronald, in the first successful kidney transplant from a live donor.

Five-month-old Siamese twins joined at the head are separated by surgery at John Gaston Hospital in Memphis, Tennessee, but one dies a few hours later.

LESS SURGERY, PLEASE

Dr. Clyde L. Randall of Buffalo, New York issues a caution to physicians against the growing tendency toward removing ovaries of women over 50.

IS THIS THE ONLY CHANNEL I CAN GET?

At a meeting of the American Association for the Advancement of Science, a Chicago doctor reveals "neuro-muscular television," an apparatus that gives the nervous heart patient a visible record of the muscle and nerve tension.

•

Dr. F.J. Stare of Harvard University concludes that the best way to treat atherosclerosis is to prevent or correct overweight.

•

The Journal of the American Medical Association reports that exercise can't hurt a normal heart and in cases where death occurs during or shortly after exercise, a preexisting heart condition is usually the cause of death.

•

KEEP ON MOVIN' ON

A study of 31,000 employees of transportation companies in Great Britain concludes that workers whose duties require walking have less coronary disease than sedentary motormen and engineers.

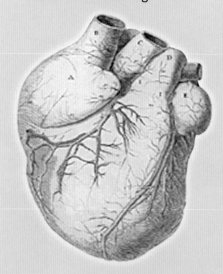

POLIO
NEWS

The number of this year's new polio cases is the third highest on record—40,000, with about half of them paralytic.

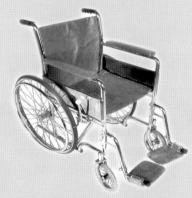

The National Foundation for Infantile Paralysis announces that a nationwide test of the Salk anti-poliomyelitis vaccine, which eventually will involve 900,000 children, has begun in several southern, western and eastern states with inoculations beginning in Pittsburgh, Pennsylvania. Volunteers for the largest U.S. peacetime mobilization ever include 20,000 doctors, 40,000 nurses and 50,000 teachers.

•

The Association for Research in Nervous & Mental Disease announces that according to test results, polio's crippling form will be eradicated when susceptible age groups are vaccinated.

•

A second polio vaccine is developed by Chicago's Michael Reese Medical Research Institute which uses "killed" polio virus, therefore making it safer for use.

•

BLONDS MAY BE HAVING MORE FUN AFTER ALL

A study of 1,183 polio victims reveals that only one patient has blond hair, blue eyes and fair skin.

NUMBER OF DOCTORS LICENSED IN THE U.S. 218,522

PHYSICIAN, STOP KILLING THYSELF!

Therapeutic Notes reports that the suicide rate for physicians is 4% higher than the average, with physicians in the military experiencing mental illness 1 1/2 to 2 times more frequently than others in the military.

THERE REALLY IS A DOCTOR IN THE HOUSE!

According to the AMA, there is now a record ratio of one doctor for every 730 inhabitants of the U.S.

REPEAT AFTER ME: BEDPANS CAN BE FUN

A physician at Cornell University observes that many hospital workers are callous and seldom make the patient feel at ease.

IF YOU'RE BLACK GET BACK; IF YOU'RE WHITE YOU'RE ALL RIGHT

The North Carolina Medical Society rejects a proposal to admit black doctors on the grounds they would "seek to capitalize on their privileges and try to mix socially with whites."

But...

The Medical Society of Virginia votes to admit black doctors as members if they are first admitted to local and county medical societies.

IT'S ALL IN THE HANDS

Here's what doctors at a Staten Island hospital report on their research of hands as a source of diagnostic information:

HAND CONDITION	POSSIBLE DIAGNOSIS
Flabby, wet and cold	Neurosis
Sweaty palm and tremor of fingers	Circulation problem
Tobacco-stained fingers with chewed-off nails	Neurosis
Bluish-colored fingers	Heart defect
Pale, waxy white palms	Anemia
Flushed	Overactive thyroid
Dry, rough, cold	Underactive thyroid
Small areas of intense coloring resembling freckles	Addison's disease

135

A professor of biochemistry at Cornell University Medical College successfully synthesizes a hormone of the pituitary gland.

Two Danish doctors report in *Postgraduate Medicine* that serious hemorrhages in newborn babies can be reduced almost 25% by giving the mothers vitamin K before delivery.

NO MORE TYPHOID MARYS

The Michigan State Health Laboratories announce the development of a new antibiotic called "synnematin" for treatment of typhoid fever.

I'D STILL LIKE TO BITE THAT NUTTY SQUIRREL BACK

Lederle Laboratories has developed a new rabies serum that gives immediate protection.

INSTANT TEST FOR SUGAR OVERLOAD

A pocket kit for a quick blood-sugar test is developed by a husband-and-wife team at Miles-Ames Laboratory in Elkhart, Indiana.

Chicago's Cook County Hospital is testing a new "slow drip" peptic ulcer pill that keeps acid-neutralizing compounds in the stomach at all times.

Terramycin is a new one-shot cure for gonorrhea, according to an article published in *Antibiotics and Chemotherapy*.

STICK THAT IN YOUR OWN EAR

A new electronic thermometer gives accurate temperature reading in five to seven seconds.

SEEING IS BELIEVING

Dr. John O'Neill of the Pennsylvania State College of Optometry reports the development of the first cornea-size contact lenses.

A University of Tennessee surgeon tells the American Medical Association that routine chest X-rays detect early and curable lung cancer.

A University of Colorado radiologist has developed an ultrasonic device that may detect hidden cancer in the form of tumors, goiters and cysts not visible with current diagnostic technology.

The Cohn blood fractionation machine, which extracts disease-killing compounds from human blood, has been perfected and is ready for use after 20 years of research led by the late Dr. Edwin J. Cohn at Harvard University.

WHAT A YEAR IT WAS!

MENTAL ILLS

Edvard Munch, *The Scream*. Lithograph, 1895

According to the National Association for Mental Health, U.S. mental hospitals care for 750,000 people a day.

At a meeting of 16 southern governors in Boca Raton, Florida, Tennessee governor Frank G. Clement asserts that no southern state has appropriated enough money to provide adequate therapeutic treatment in its mental institutions.

The Chicago Institute for Psychoanalysis says that women are doing very well as professional psychologists and attributes their success to their natural empathic abilities.

THE EVER-EMERGING NEW YOU

A visiting professor of psychology at UCLA says that your personality can change as it is influenced by new goals, marriage, business or life's experiences.

An article appearing in the CHICAGO DAILY TRIBUNE absolves nerves as a cause of stomach ulcers, but states that nerves play a big part in the duodenal-type ulcer.

SHOCK CAN LEAD TO LOSS OF SHOCKS

A report to the Medical Society of the State of Pennsylvania supports the popular idea that shock or sudden grief can cause baldness as well as loss of eyebrows, eyelashes and underarm hair.

 ## RICH MEN'S JUSTICE

A UCLA criminologist says wealthy shoplifters are called "kleptomaniacs" while poor shoplifters are called "thieves."

THE CONSTANT ROLLS IN THE HAY WON'T DO IT

The Don Juan type of male, who typically has sex with a great number of women, is characterized by a UCLA psychiatrist as being anxious and insecure about his masculinity and needs repeated sexual experiences to prove that he is masculine.

A survey of sex offenders conducted at UCLA reveals that the average sex offender is actually shy, introverted and religious and not the stereotype of a brutal, violent maniac.

A BRAINY SUBJECT

A Yale University scientist reports a new technique of controlling the brain electrically by implanting electrodes in the brain that could reveal some of the mysteries surrounding this most vital organ.

IN SEARCH OF A **MIGHTY BIG COUCH**

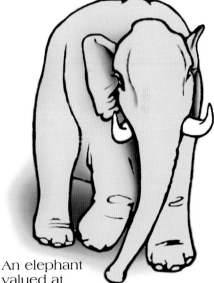

An elephant valued at $5,600 is being sent to the U.S. from India to be psycho-analyzed because of her refusal to be around children.

THE LITTLE ANIMALS THAT WEREN'T

Many serious highway accidents are caused when truck drivers try to avoid hitting an animal that actually isn't there because of hallucinations generally caused by lack of sleep.

YOUR HEALTH UP IN SMOKE, OR SMOKE NOW, PAY LATER

A report to the British House of Commons establishes that based on statistical evidence, there is a relationship between smoking and lung cancer.

THERE IS A SMOKING GUN

For the first time, the American Cancer Society says that smoking unequivocally hastens death through lung cancer and coronary heart disease.

• According to an article published in the JOURNAL OF THE STATE MEDICAL SOCIETY, men who smoke 20 or more cigarettes a day have 10 times more cases of lung cancer than non-smokers.

• A survey of 187,766 men between 50 to 70 years of age, taken over 2 1/2 years by the American Cancer Society, shows a substantially higher death rate among smokers than among non-smokers or those who use pipes or cigars.

• The American Cancer Society says smokers over 50 have a 75% higher death rate.

• The Public Health Cancer Association's executive board votes 13-3 to recommend that Americans stop smoking cigarettes because there is sufficient evidence available of a relationship between cigarette smoking and lung cancer.

• A report submitted to the American Cancer Society by 25 researchers states that the evidence justifies the suspicion that cigarette smoking does, to a degree as yet undetermined, increase the likelihood of developing lung cancer.

MEANWHILE, BACK IN THE BACK OFFICE...

Tobacco companies form a Tobacco Industry Commission to get the facts about some doctors' contention that smoking contributes to lung cancer.

The Tobacco Industry issues a pamphlet citing statements by 36 cancer specialists to support their contention that there is "no proof that cigarette smoking is a cause of lung cancer."

DON'T HOLD YOUR BREATH

Doing five-minute breathing exercises 8 to 10 times a day helped 15 heavy smokers kick the habit according to a report published in the JOURNAL OF THE AMERICAN MEDICAL ASSOCIATION.

Number of Social Drinkers in the U.S.

60 million

I'LL HAVE A DOUBLE CREAM SODA IN A BUCKET— ONE ONION

A research assistant in sociology at Yale explains that the reason alcoholism is rare among Jewish people is because alcohol is part of their religious ritual and is consumed with the family, and the pressures on them as a minority group call for sobriety.

WHAT A YEAR IT WAS!

NOW...A REVOLUTIONARY NEW KIND OF COUGH REMEDY!

Like a Doctor's Cough Prescription

(<u>Combines</u> three highly effective cough medicines)

in chewing-gum form

MEDIGUM For Coughs DUE TO COLDS

COUGHING? START CHEWING!

.....IN TASTY CHEWING-GUM FORM

CONTAINS TERPIN HYDRATE—A WIDELY PRESCRIBED COUGH MEDICINE

16 FOR 35¢

Each **MEDIGUM** tablet gives you **more** medicine—and more **effective** medicine—than a **whole teaspoonful** of a widely prescribed cough remedy.

Stops raspy throat "tickle" almost instantly

Penetrates to cold-irritated throat tissues better than syrups, gargles

Loosens phlegm, eases chest "tightness"—deep-down relief!

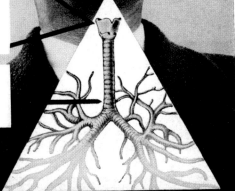

Wonderful Relief for "Smoker's Cough"

Like to *smoke*—but hate to *cough?* Chew good-tasting MEDIGUM—carry it as you do cigarettes, cigars or your pipe. Feel the difference in your throat as MEDIGUM soothes away "Smoker's Cough" irritation.

Deep-Down <u>Medicinal</u> Relief for

Coughs Throat Irritations DUE TO COLDS

Now no need to be tortured by nagging coughs due to colds—or raspy, cold-irritated throat! For wonderful deep-down *medicinal* relief—relief that *starts in seconds*—just chew amazing new MEDIGUM!

Like a doctor's cough prescription, MEDIGUM gives you the comforting action of not just one but *three* effective cough medicines . . . in *handy chewing-gum form.*

Medicates as You Chew

As you chew new MEDIGUM, a *continuing* medicated bath instantly moistens and soothes dry, raspy throat—stops "tickle". Quickly relieves cold-irritated throat tissues that cough syrups and gargles may not even touch! And in coughs due to colds, MEDIGUM works deep-down . . . loosens bronchial phlegm . . . eases chest "tightness". Relief is amazing—you feel better faster!

Delicious—Easy to Take

MEDIGUM tastes delicious. Chew it at home, at work, while driving a car. For the good of your whole family, get new MEDIGUM at any drug counter—today!

RECOMMENDED FOR CHILDREN

MEDIGUM is ideal for children as well as grown-ups. They take it gladly, when needed, because it tastes so good. And it doesn't upset even delicate digestions . . . doesn't spoil appetites like sugary syrups.

Just CHEW...any time, any place!

Whenever, wherever you cough . . . MEDIGUM in your pocket or purse offers on-the-spot relief. Carry it with you . . . working, playing, at the movies, when you travel. Chew *convenient* MEDIGUM and get *real medicinal* cough relief!

MEDIGUM

PHARMACO, INC., KENILWORTH, N. J.

16 TABLETS 35¢

TEENAGE Fears

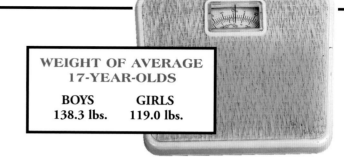

WEIGHT OF AVERAGE 17-YEAR-OLDS	
BOYS	GIRLS
138.3 lbs.	119.0 lbs.

(97 first-year students of an Oregon High School)

Fear of the dark

Feelings of personal inadequacy

Fear of not being liked

Fear of criticism

Fear of not handling problems well

Fear of drunks, strangers and kidnappers

Fear of cars

Fear of heights

Fear of water

Fear of injury

Fear of the opposite sex

Fear of dating

Fear of parents

A MARKED CONCLUSION

According to two doctors at Albany Medical College, birthmarks occur twice as frequently in girls as in boys.

STICK WITH THE MILK, KID

According to a study published in the *Quarterly Review of Pediatrics*, the current trend of introducing solid food to babies finds little or no enthusiasm from leading pediatricians.

THAT'S NOT A TEST TUBE, THAT'S YOUR DADDY

Iowa University reports the first three births of babies whose mothers were artificially inseminated with stored frozen semen.

COULD BE ALL GREEK TO BABY

Calling the learning of languages the human brain's first miracle, the director of the Montreal Neurological Institute suggests that children learn additional languages when they are young.

SMART AT FINALS

A professor at Stanford University recommends that the exceptionally gifted child should be spotted early and allowed to speed through her grade school and high school education so that she can enter college by 16 or 17.

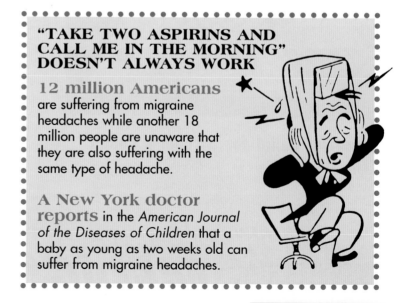

"TAKE TWO ASPIRINS AND CALL ME IN THE MORNING" DOESN'T ALWAYS WORK

12 million Americans are suffering from migraine headaches while another 18 million people are unaware that they are also suffering with the same type of headache.

A New York doctor reports in the *American Journal of the Diseases of Children* that a baby as young as two weeks old can suffer from migraine headaches.

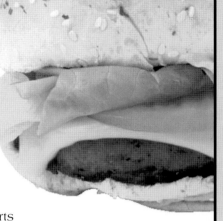

EAT NOW, CLOG LATER

There is evidence that eating large amounts of fatty foods contributes to hardening of the arteries.

A SALTY SUBJECT

Low-salt milk is being made available to heart patients in Los Angeles.

FEELING TENSE?
EAT A PLANT

The National Heart Institute reports that a hypertension drug is being brewed from fresh leaves of the rhododendron plant.

BRING ON THE YOGURT AND ORANGES

The diet of most women over 30 is deficient in milk and foods containing vitamin C.

DIE #10

Dr. Ree Trauhaut of the University of Paris, along with doctors from six European nations, ask that dyes and other substances known to cause cancer in test animals be barred from human food. Dr. Willard E. Smith of NYU-Bellevue Medical Center says that with the approval of the Food & Drug Administration, 100,000 pounds of such material was used in human food in the U.S. last year.

FUNGUS IN THE RYE

According to a New York doctor, people who eat too much rye bread run the risk of developing Buerger's disease, a serious ailment of the blood vessels in the legs brought on by a fungus that is found in rye bread.

MINERALS
THAT SHOULD BE IN YOUR DIET
(According to the Nutrition Foundation)

Calcium
Phosphorus
Magnesium
Sodium
Potassium
Chlorine
Sulfur
Iron
Copper
Cobalt
Iodine
Manganese
Zinc
Fluorine
Molybdenum

The Illinois State Medical Society issues a warning on the dangers of putting oneself on a low-salt or salt-free diet, saying that it's potentially harmful to upset the salt balance of the body.

THIS MAY HURT HIM AS MUCH AS IT HURTS YOU

A study conducted with 56 dentists at the Newark Clinical Group reveals that a state of anxiety is the most common condition found among dentists.

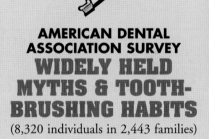

AMERICAN DENTAL ASSOCIATION SURVEY
WIDELY HELD MYTHS & TOOTH-BRUSHING HABITS
(8,320 individuals in 2,443 families)

80%
believe pregnancy is cause of tooth decay.

69.7%
believe eating foods with vitamins and minerals will prevent tooth decay.

63.4%
believe the fetus absorbs calcium from the mother's teeth.

49%
of housewives brush twice a day.

7%
brush once a day.

4%
know teeth should be brushed immediately after eating.

NOBEL PRIZES

CHEMISTRY
Linus Pauling
(USA)

PHYSIOLOGY or MEDICINE
John F. Enders
(USA)
Frederick C. Robbins
(USA)
Thomas H. Weller
(USA)

PHYSICS
Max Born
(Great Britain)
Walther Bothe
(West Germany)

Asserting that there is little chance of hormones causing cancer, a clinical professor of medicine at UCLA suggests that women past middle age be given small amounts of female hormones to postpone the aging of skin, bones and reproductive organs.

THIS IS DEFINITELY GOING TO HURT YOU MORE THAN HIM

Using a revolving steel brush operated like a dental drill, "planing," a new technique for removing scars caused by acne or accidents, is being tested.

WHAT A YEAR IT WAS!

According to recent studies, fat men get less cold than their skinny counterparts.

The *Journal of the American Medical Association* lists safety rules for your summer vacation:

- **Do not go outdoors during thunderstorms.**
- **On hot days, drink water regularly, whether you're thirsty or not.**
- **Work or sleep in an air-conditioned room to prevent prickly heat.**
- **If you contract poison ivy, use cortisone and hydrocortisone to halt the itching.**

WARNING: WASHING DISHES COULD BE DETRIMENTAL TO YOUR SKIN

It is reported that about one out of every 10 patients seeing a dermatologist has skin inflammation, with most of them being housewives.

CURBING YOUR NEED FOR HELP

The New York University engineering college has developed a simple wheelchair that allows a patient to climb street curbs without the aid of another person.

AH CHOO – GESUNDHEIT

The chairman of the pollen survey committee of the American Academy of Allergy advises that ragweed sufferers avoid the Midwest during hay fever season.

WARMING UP THOSE OLD BONES

A Boston doctor concludes that May is the best month for arthritics.

NUMBER OF PEOPLE IN THE U.S. SUFFERING FROM ARTHRITIS AND RHEUMATISM

10 million (over age 14)

SLOW BOAT TO CHINA?

An editorial in the *Journal of the American Medical Association* says that when you have an urge to get away from it all, you probably should, as it's a sign of stress and time to take therapeutic measures.

JUST DON'T ROCK THE BOAT

An article in the *Annals of Allergy* reports that dramamine, used to combat seasickness, is found to relieve nausea caused by migraine headaches.

READ & HEAL

The University of Iowa hospital reports success in healing patients by having them read books as part of a treatment to relax patients and divert their attention away from their ailments.

DOES THIS INCLUDE SHUFFLEBOARD?

How to stay young? Be creative, use your inner resources, have a hobby and participate in group activities.

I See From This Squiggle That You'd Like To Fly Away

An article appearing in the *International Record of Medicine and General Practice Clinics* states that graphology or the study of handwriting can be useful in uncovering a patient's emotions.

WHAT A YEAR IT WAS!

Start of a perfect day...

THE MODERN WAY TO ACCOUNTING!

A joy from start to finish, Burroughs Sensimatic cuts today's rising accounting costs effectively, economically. That's because Sensimatic has the *exclusive* sensing panel that permits this versatile accounting machine to do so many jobs in a new way. Just a turn of the selector knob converts the Sensimatic from one accounting operation to another—a single machine can handle a wide range of applications, simply and easily ... without extensive operator training.

Choose from five great series of Sensimatics. Contact your nearest Burroughs branch. Burroughs Corporation, Detroit 32, Michigan.

Burroughs Sensimatic

Burroughs **B**

BUSINESS

1954

The Gross National Product is $356 billion.

Unemployment hovers around 3.3 million people.

The national debt for fiscal 1954 is $271,260,000,000.

The average workweek is 39 hours. 45% of manufacturing employees work a 40-hour workweek, 20% work under 40 hours and 35% work over 40 hours.

A good job is almost a certain thing for 1954 college grads with degrees in business, engineering and accounting.

Corporate dividends reach a record high of $9.3 billion.

53,000 Eastman Kodak workers split $28.5 million in dividends.

THE BANKING BIZ

Bank of California, California Bank and Crocker First National Bank merge, with combined assets of over $1 billion.

There are over 500 mutual savings banks in the U.S.

Commercial loan interest rates hover around 3%.

The Housing Act allows people with mortgages insured by the Federal Housing Administration to take up to 30 years to pay off the loan.

SHOP 'TIL YOU DROP

NORTHLAND MALL opens outside Detroit, instantly becoming both the first shopping mall in America and the largest shopping center in the world.

SEARS, ROEBUCK AND COMPANY begins selling appliances by outside manufacturers while keeping its house brand, Kenmore.

GENERAL ELECTRIC forgoes recommended list prices on major appliances such as refrigerators and washing machines, realizing customers rarely pay full price anymore.

PAN AMERICAN WORLD AIRWAYS becomes the first U.S. airline to offer customers a way to travel by using a payment plan with only 10% down.

DIAMONDS ARE A GIRL'S BEST FRIEND

The diamond trade booms as federal excise taxes are reduced from 20% to 10%.

Sales of hard coal are slumping, forcing mines to slash prices up to 12%.

WHAT A YEAR IT WAS!

FOOD FACTS

Multimixer wholesaler **Ray Kroc** visits the **McDonald's** hamburger stand in San Bernardino, California, where the McDonald brothers use eight of his milk-shake makers at the same time. Kroc suggests opening more restaurants.

General Foods ends its 1954 fiscal year with an all-time high of $783 million in sales.

Two of the biggest names in food come together to thrive in the Canadian baking market. The **Kellogg Company** and **Pillsbury Mills** start the **Kellogg-Pillsbury Company of Canada** to get ahead in the marketplace before competitor **General Mills** succeeds.

Soda maker **Coca-Cola** accounts for approximately 50% of all U.S. soft drink sales. Rival **Pepsi-Cola** garners about 12% of the soda-sipping market.

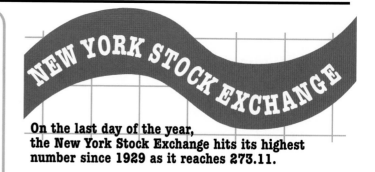

NEW YORK STOCK EXCHANGE

On the last day of the year, the New York Stock Exchange hits its highest number since 1929 as it reaches 273.11.

573,374,622 shares are traded on the New York Stock Exchange, the most since 1933.

Some of the New York Stock Exchange's most popular stocks are:

American Gas & Electric
American Telephone & Telegraph
Dow Chemical
E.I. du Pont
General Electric
General Motors
Gulf Oil
Kennecott Copper
Phillips Petroleum
RCA
Sears, Roebuck and Company
Socony-Vacuum
Standard Oil (NJ)
Standard Oil of California
Texas Company
Union Carbide
Westinghouse Electric

VROOM, VROOM

The market share of American cars breaks down as follows:

General Motors	49.9%
Ford Motor Company	30.8%
Chrysler Corporation	13.5%
Others	5.8%

Chrysler, and thus parent company General Motors, wins an Army contract worth over $160 million.

Ford introduces the Thunderbird.

A Corvette becomes the 50 millionth car to be made in a General Motors factory. The lucky town? Flint, Michigan.

47 million automobiles grace American roadways.

MERGING, MERGING, MERGING. . .
Packard Motor Car Company and Studebaker Corporation merge, becoming Studebaker-Packard Corporation.

KEEP THOSE COMPANIES MERGING. . .
Nash-Kelvinator Corporation and Hudson Motor Car Company merge, becoming American Motors Corporation.

STRIKES

CIO UNITED STEELWORKERS OF AMERICA sign a two-year, no strike agreement with U.S. Steel Corporation. Between the hourly raise of 5¢ and other benefits, the average raise for union members reaches 12¢ an hour. Other major steel companies follow suit.

CIO UNITED STEELWORKERS OF AMERICA strike for 42 days against 40 American Can Company plants. The workers win an 8 1/2 ¢ an hour raise plus additional benefits.

IN DETROIT, a work stoppage turns violent as 1,200 United Electrical Workers and CIO United Auto Workers strike against the Square D Electrical Company.

25,500 CIO UNITED RUBBER WORKERS strike against eight Firestone Tire & Rubber plants and win a 6 1/2 ¢ an hour raise.

23,000 CIO UNITED RUBBER WORKERS strike against 10 Goodyear plants for 51 days, the first time the company has been affected by a strike.

25,000 MEMBERS OF THE INTERNATIONAL LONGSHOREMEN'S ASSOCIATION strike for one day around New York ports. They win a retroactive 8¢ an hour raise.

4,500 WORKERS at the Oak Ridge, Tennessee atomic plant win a retroactive 6¢ an hour raise, with more promised next year.

A CLASH WITH AMERICAN AIRLINES over forced retirement of stewardesses at age 32 brings about an appeal to the National Mediation Board by the Air Line Stewards and Stewardesses Association.

OVER 1,200 AMERICAN AIRLINES PILOTS strike for several weeks, grounding hundreds of flights. The pilots were protesting 8-hour, 35-minute nonstop flights without a change of personnel.

SCREEN EXTRAS GUILD and the Association of Motion Picture Producers agree on salary increases for guild members. The pay for extras is boosted to a daily rate of $19.43, while stand-ins receive $18.85.

A YEAR-OLD STRIKE against many Pittsburgh department stores including Gimbels and Rosenbaum's by AFL General Teamsters Union deliverymen ends with the union gaining a 5¢ an hour raise with more to come.

WITHOUT A STRIKE, approximately 100,000 CIO International Electrical Workers receive a pay raise of 4-8¢ an hour from General Electric.

A strike against Hat Corporation of America by 1,500 AFL United Hat, Cap and Millinery Workers ends after 10 1/2 months.

HOTEL NEWS

The Fontainebleau Hotel opens on Miami Beach's Millionaire's Row.

The nation's largest hotel chain, Hilton Hotels, grows even larger as it pays $111 million for Hotel Statler Company's eight hotels (plus two under construction). For $1.4 million, New York's Astor Hotel becomes the 30th hotel in the Sheraton chain.

PASSINGS

Paul Braniff, 54
Founder and first pilot of Braniff Airways.

Clyde Cessna, 74
Airplane maker and aviation legend.

Bertie Forbes, 73
Originator of *Forbes* magazine.

Jay Hormel, 61
Creator of the mystery meat, Spam.

John Josiah Newberry, 76
Retailer who began the J.J. Newberry five-and-dime chain of stores.

Albert Plesman, 64
KLM Royal Dutch Airlines founder and chairman of the board.

WHAT A YEAR IT WAS!

1954

1954
This Is THE PRICE THAT WAS

FOOD BASKET

Angel Food Cake	$ .68
Apples (lb.)	.12
Avocados (each)	.19
Bananas (lb.)	.10
Bread (loaf)	.17
Butter (lb.)	.65
Cabbage (lb.)	.03
Cake Mix	.29
Candy Bar	.05
Cantaloupe (lb.)	.05
Carrots (bunch)	.03
Cherries (lb.)	.19
Coffee (lb.)	.89
Cola	.05
Cottage Cheese (pt.)	.20
Cucumbers (each)	.04
Dates (lb.)	.19
Eggs (doz.)	.49
Grapes (lb.)	.17
Green Beans (lb.)	.10
Lemons (lb.)	.09
Lettuce (head)	.05
Milk (qt.)	.20
Oranges (lb.)	.06
Pancake Syrup	.29
Peanut Butter	.39
Pears (lb.)	.10
Potato Chips	.39
Sugar (lb.)	.10
Swiss Cheese (lb.)	.59
Watermelon (each)	.39
Yams (lb.)	.08

YEARLY SALARIES

Jackie Gleason	$11,000,000
(2-year television contract)	
Clark Gable	$500,000
Attorney	$7,500
Electronic Engineer	$7,500
Hairdresser	$5,200
Pastry Chef	$4,900
Railroad Worker	$4,500
IBM Tab Operator	$3,600
Teacher	$3,500
Bookkeeper	$3,400
Stenographer	$3,100
Switchboard Operator	$2,900
Bank Guard	$2,600
Receptionist	$2,300
Messenger	$2,100
Farm Worker	$1,500

Jackie Gleason

HOME SWEET HOME

3-Bedroom House

Santa Monica, CA	$15,900
Skokie, IL	$18,500
San Fernando Valley, CA	$18,950
Brooklyn, NY	$19,750
Teaneck, NJ	$23,490
Bucks County, PA	$26,000
Stamford, CT	$28,000
Orlando, FL	$31,000
Scarsdale, NY	$40,000

148

WHAT A YEAR IT WAS!

ODDS & ENDS

Bobby Pins	$	.25
Child Care (hourly)		.40
Children's Bicycle		40.88
Hotel Room, Essex House, NY		9.00
MG Series TF Car		1,995.00
Monopoly Game		4.00
Movie Theatre Admission		.50
Phone Calls (3 minutes):		
NY - Philadelphia		.40
Chicago - Omaha		.85
Philadelphia - Miami		1.35
SF - Boston		2.00
Playing Cards		.49
Polaroid Camera		89.75
Speeding Ticket, England		5.60

THIS OLD HOUSE

Air Conditioner	$ 199.95
Aluminum Foil	.21
Aspirin	.69
Crib	24.98
Dishwasher	239.50
Iron	13.95
Laundry Detergent	.30
Paper Napkins	.10
Phonograph	29.95
Refrigerator	154.00
Toaster	23.95
TV (21″)	289.95
Umbrella	2.77
Vacuum Cleaner	69.99
Washing Machine	239.95
Wheelbarrow	11.88

STOCKS

20th Century Fox	27 7/8
AT&T	172 1/8
Boeing Aircraft	62
Decca Records	14 1/2
Dow Chemical	41 1/8
Firestone	82 1/2
IBM	287 1/2
Motorola	45
Pitney Bowes	32 1/2
RCA	34 1/4
Rexall Drugs	6 7/8
Safeway Stores	44 1/2
Sears, Roebuck	73 1/2
Shell Oil	57 1/2
Studebaker-Packard	13 1/8
Wamsutta	9 1/2

A seat on the New York Stock Exchange sells for $70,000.

LA BOUTIQUE

Men's Oxford Shirt	$ 10.50
Men's Shoes	18.95
Men's Silk Tie	1.95
Men's Stetson Hat	10.00
Women's Girdle	3.99
Women's Linen Suit	49.95
Women's Shoes	16.95

TRAVEL

Plane Tickets:	
LA - NY (r/t)	$ 160.00
LA - SF (o/w)	27.00
LA - Chicago (r/t)	140.00
Train, LA to Chicago (o/w)	55.44

WHAT A YEAR IT WAS!

DISASTERS

USA

541 people die from drowning, car accidents and fireworks during the 4th of July holiday weekend.

Traffic fatalities over the New Year's holiday reach over 300 deaths.

Deadly fumes follow a factory explosion and fire, killing nine firemen in the line of duty in Philadelphia.

Over 250 people die in the Midwest and Southwest, along with many livestock deaths and severe crop damage, during a two-week heat wave.

Hurricane Carol hits the East Coast, causing 68 deaths and approximately $500 million in property damage. Rhode Island and Massachusetts are severely hit, while damage is also caused in New Hampshire, New York, New Jersey, Virginia, Delaware, Connecticut, Maine and parts of Quebec, Canada.

Driving rains cause the Chicago River to flood parts of the city's business district, bringing about 14 deaths and $25 million in damage.

Approximately 251 U.S. servicemen die in airplane crashes both on U.S. soil and abroad.

Europe

45 coal miners die in an explosion at Chorzow, Poland.

In January, nearly 200 die during avalanches in the Alps, while 166 mountaineers perish during the Alps' summer climbing season.

A trolley accident kills 17 in Zagreb, Yugoslavia.

WHAT A YEAR IT WAS!

Caribbean

A landslide destroys the entire town of Berly, Haiti. 260 people are presumed dead.

Central America

47 people are killed when a bus plummets off a cliff near Guatemala City, Guatemala.

Asia

As many as 500 Hindu pilgrims die and 2,000 are injured at Allahabad, India during a rush to bathe in the Ganges during the Kumbha Mela celebration.

Flooding causes the Panchen Lama's palace in Shigatse, Tibet to collapse, killing approximately 200 people.

Between monsoon-caused landslides and floods in two separate areas of Nepal, an estimated 900 people are killed.

Nearly 1,600 people are confirmed dead on and around Hokkaido Island, Japan after a typhoon causes floods, fires, landslides and boats to sink. Fatalities from the ferryboat *Toya Maru* reach nearly 1,200.

Africa

Earthquakes in Northern Algeria kill over 1,600 people, injure 2,500 and leave about 10,000 people without homes.

Middle East

Istanbul's nearly 500-year-old bazaar sustains nearly $180 million in fire damage. Approximately 2,000 shops are destroyed, as are many of the bazaar's old pathways.

N.Y. Yankees At Training Camp

Casey **Stengel** *(left)* and **George Weiss** take a close look at the Yankees as they go through their training.

Old Casey is looking ahead to a sixth straight world championship.

But before then there are a few questions to ask, like "Who's on first?" Is it *(from top)* **Joe Collins**, **Bill Skowron** or **Frank Leja**? Or will it be **Eddie Robinson**, native of Philadelphia, wearing that old number 36 now that **Johnny Mize** is retired?

But the champs are still knee-deep in talent and the team to beat. **Hank Bauer** *(from left)* is back as are **Yogi Berra** and **Gene Woodling**. **Gil McDougald** adds more power to a powerful lineup.

Bill Dickey *(left)* gives a few pointers to rookie **Elston Howard**, the first black player on the team.

As for the pitching staff, there's **Whitey Ford**, 18-game winner last year *(far left)*, and **Allie Reynolds**, looking for another good year himself.

From Philadelphia, the Yanks acquired the big right-hander **Harry Byrd** *(bottom left)*. Question: Will Byrd fill the shoes of **Vic Raschi** *(bottom center)*, who was sold to the Cardinals in one of the big surprise deals of the winter?

If longtime Yank Raschi has a good year, the Yankees might regret the sale, but Cardinal manager **Eddie Stanky** *(bottom right)* would be glad indeed. But time will tell.

BASEBALL ● NEWS

World Series
New York Giants over Cleveland Indians, 4-0

⚾ The St. Louis Browns become the Baltimore Orioles.

⚾ **Willie Mays** executes a spectacular over-the-shoulder catch of a **Vic Wertz** fly ball in Game One of the 1954 World Series.

⚾ **Stan Musial** sets a major-league record for home runs in a double-header by hitting 5 against the N.Y. Giants in St. Louis.

⚾ N.Y. Giants complete the World Series sweep of the Indians as **Don Liddle** beats **Bob Lemon**, 7-4. Cleveland's season record of 111-43 sets an American League mark for regular season wins.

⚾ During an exhibition game against the Yankees, newly acquired Brave **Bobby Thomson** breaks his ankle. The '51 National League playoff hero is replaced by a promising prospect named **Hank Aaron**.

⚾ In an exhibition game against the Red Sox, **Hank Aaron** gets three hits in his first start as a Brave.

⚾ In a 9-8 victory over the Braves, Reds **Jim Greengrass** hits four doubles in his major-league debut while **Hank Aaron** goes hitless in five attempts in his first major-league game.

⚾ Baltimore's Memorial Stadium opens as a crowd of 46,354 watches the Orioles beat the White Sox, 3-1.

⚾ In his seventh major-league game, Braves outfielder **Hank Aaron** hits his home run off Cardinal hurler **Vic Raschi**.

⚾ The Philadelphia A's and St. Louis Cardinals set a major-league record using 42 players in one game. Philadelphia wins game in 11 innings, 14-10.

⚾ The Major League Baseball Players Association is organized in Cleveland in order to represent players in policy-making negotiations with club owners.

⚾ Blacks play with whites in Memphis for the first time when the American League Chicago White Sox use outfielders **Minnie Minoso** and **Bob Boyd** in an exhibition game against the National League St. Louis Cardinals.

⚾ **Red Barber** becomes baseball announcer for New York Yankees.

The **ALL-AMERICAN GIRLS** Professional Baseball League, in which hundreds of women participated since its 1943 inception, disbands.

For the first time in major-league baseball, a majority of a team's starting lineup is made up of black players: Jim Gilliam, Jackie Robinson, Sandy Amoros, Roy Campanella and Don Newcombe (Brooklyn Dodgers).

WHO'S GETTING THE BIG BUCKS
(Baseball Contracts)
Approximate

Jackie Robinson
$40,000
(Brooklyn Dodgers)

•

Red Schoendienst
$50,000
(St. Louis Cardinals)

•

Stan Musial*
$80,000
(St. Louis Cardinals)

•

Roy Campanella
$35,000
(Brooklyn Dodgers)

•

Yogi Berra
$41,000
(N.Y. Yankees)

•

Bob Lemon**
$42,000
(Cleveland Indians)

*highest salary in National League history
**highest-paid American League pitcher

NEW STATISTIC:
Sacrifice Flies

Home Run Leaders
National League
Ted Kluszewski (Cincinnati, 49)
American League
Larry Doby (Cleveland, 32)

Batting Champions
National League
Willie Mays (New York, .345)
American League
Bobby Avila (Cleveland, .341)

Most Valuable Player
National League
Willie Mays (New York)
American League
Yogi Berra (New York)

Strikeouts
National League
Robin Roberts (Philadelphia, 185)
American League
Bob Turley (Baltimore, 185)

Rookie Of The Year
National League
Wally Moon (St. Louis)
American League
Bob Grim (New York)

All-Star Game
American over National, 11-9
Casey Stengel, American manager
Walter Alston, National manager

WHAT A YEAR IT WAS!

Willie Mays Back In Action

N.Y. Giants manager Leo Durocher *(far left)* and his coaching staff are all smiles.

48-year-old Durocher is named "Manager of the Year" by AP polls of sportswriters.

The reason they're happy? It's the return from army service of the very popular **Willie Mays**, who is expected by many fans to do more for the team than any single player.

On the mound, expected to add new and needed pitching strength, are rookies *(from left)* **Jim Constable** and **Windy McCall** with **Johnny Antonelli** and **Don Liddle** obtained from the Braves for **Bobby Thomson**. A hopeful year ahead.

Thing of beauty and a jo

Study this one well, good friend—then ready yourself for the high-voltage news.

This automobile—this gorgeous grace of glass and color and flowing line pictured here—is the 1954 Buick SPECIAL Convertible.

It is Buick's lowest-priced Convertible.

It sells for just a few dollars more than similar models of the so-called "low-price three."

MILTON BERLE
STARS FOR BUICK
See the
Buick-Berle Show
Tuesday Evenings

But from that point on, it differs every step of the w

It's styled to the breath of Spring and the lift of a breeze.

It's pulsed with a completely new V8 that's in the rec books as the highest-powered engine ever placed in a Bu of this budget-priced Series.

It's cradled on a chassis of 122 inches, where four coil sprin and a steadying torque-tube, and a sensational new front-e geometry give you a ride and handling ease that come pre near to bliss.

The sports-car styled 1954 Buick SPECIAL Convertible—lowest-priced of Buick's four great Series— now V8 powered for record-high performance, compression ratio, fuel economy.

r budgets

it's new, this Buick—utterly new, like every 1954 Buick.

in style, body, interior. New in the backswept expanse panoramic windshield. New in the wider swing-open of ors. New in the better fuel economy of its Power-Head is. New in a long list of advancements that add to comfort, nience and safety.

Buick dealer cordially invites you to drop in and see this ing new Buick and judge for yourself what a thrill and it is in every way. BUICK *Division of* GENERAL MOTORS

BUICK
the Beautiful Buy

WHEN BETTER AUTOMOBILES ARE BUILT BUICK WILL BUILD THEM

159

The CLEVELAND BROWNS *Meet*
The Favored DETROIT LIONS *For The*
WORLD'S PRO FOOTBALL CHAMPIONSHIP

Cleveland's **Otto Graham** (#14) connects with a 37-yard toss.

The Lions roar back at the start of the second period as **Lew Carpenter** travels 52 yards on Layne's handoff.

Bobby Layne tosses *(top)* and the Browns' **Don Paul** intercepts, taking the ball 33 yards before he's tackled *(bottom).*

Layne fades back and flips a 19-yard aerial *(top)* and a spectacular catch by **Dorne Dibble** sets up the scoring play *(bottom).*

With the Browns leading, Graham fires a pass to **Pete Brewster** *(top)*. He's down in the two and up and over for the score *(bottom).*

It's **Bill Bowman** (#33) taking the pitch out *(top)* and crossing the goal line with a score for the Lions, their last of the day *(bottom).*

WHAT A YEAR IT WAS!

Before the half, Cleveland scores two more times.

Walt Michaels (#34) intercepts a Layne pass *(top)* and takes it back 14 yards *(bottom)*.

Graham is the man again with his third touchdown pass *(top)*. A spectacular showing in the Browns' stunning 56-10 upset *(bottom)*.

NATIONAL FOOTBALL LEAGUE CHAMPIONS
Cleveland Browns
over **Detroit Lions**
56-10

MOST VALUABLE PLAYER
Joe Perry
San Francisco, FB

NFL PRO BOWL
East
over **West**
20-9

NATIONAL COLLEGE FOOTBALL CHAMPIONS
Ohio State, 10-0-0
UCLA, 9-0-0

ROSE BOWL
Michigan State
over **UCLA**
28-20

HEISMAN TROPHY
Alan Ameche
Wisconsin, FB

WHAT A YEAR IT WAS!

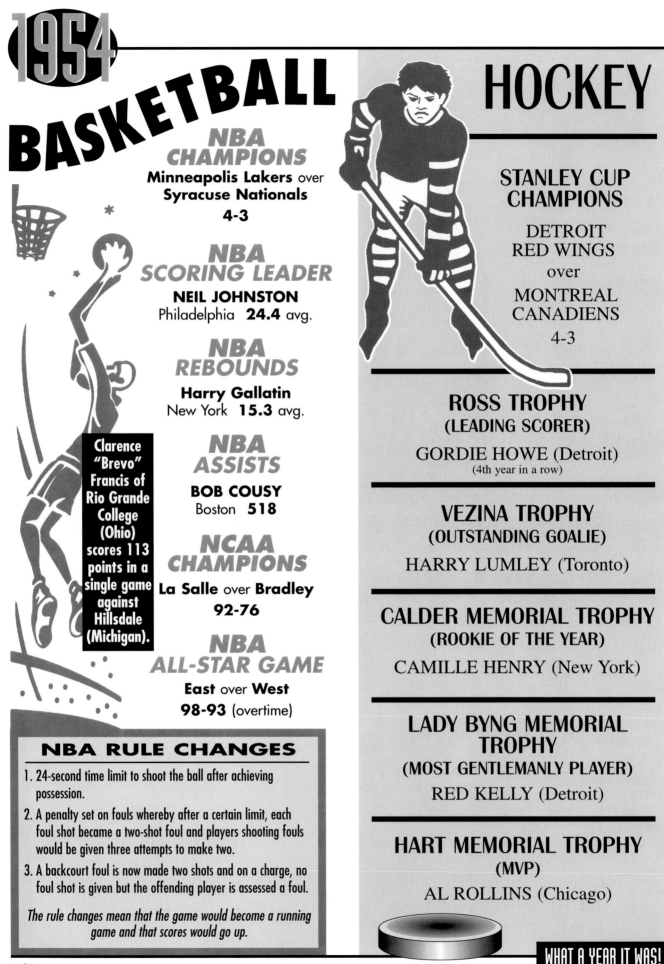

1954

BASKETBALL

NBA CHAMPIONS
Minneapolis Lakers over **Syracuse Nationals**
4-3

NBA SCORING LEADER
NEIL JOHNSTON
Philadelphia **24.4** avg.

NBA REBOUNDS
Harry Gallatin
New York **15.3** avg.

Clarence "Brevo" Francis of Rio Grande College (Ohio) scores 113 points in a single game against Hillsdale (Michigan).

NBA ASSISTS
BOB COUSY
Boston **518**

NCAA CHAMPIONS
La Salle over **Bradley**
92-76

NBA ALL-STAR GAME
East over **West**
98-93 (overtime)

NBA RULE CHANGES

1. 24-second time limit to shoot the ball after achieving possession.
2. A penalty set on fouls whereby after a certain limit, each foul shot became a two-shot foul and players shooting fouls would be given three attempts to make two.
3. A backcourt foul is now made two shots and on a charge, no foul shot is given but the offending player is assessed a foul.

The rule changes mean that the game would become a running game and that scores would go up.

HOCKEY

STANLEY CUP CHAMPIONS

DETROIT RED WINGS
over
MONTREAL CANADIENS
4-3

ROSS TROPHY
(LEADING SCORER)

GORDIE HOWE (Detroit)
(4th year in a row)

VEZINA TROPHY
(OUTSTANDING GOALIE)

HARRY LUMLEY (Toronto)

CALDER MEMORIAL TROPHY
(ROOKIE OF THE YEAR)

CAMILLE HENRY (New York)

LADY BYNG MEMORIAL TROPHY
(MOST GENTLEMANLY PLAYER)

RED KELLY (Detroit)

HART MEMORIAL TROPHY
(MVP)

AL ROLLINS (Chicago)

WHAT A YEAR IT WAS!

"Getting Ready for Christmas," by Haddon Sundblom. Number 102 in the series, "Home Life in America"

In this friendly, freedom-loving land of ours... *Beer Belongs—Enjoy It!*

BEER AND ALE—AMERICA'S BEVERAGES OF MODERATION
Sponsored by the United States Brewers Foundation . . . Chartered 1862

1954

Great names in sports from yesterday and today are honored at this gala event.

PHILADELPHIA SPORTSWRITERS' GOLDEN ANNIVERSARY CELEBRATION

Al Rosen of the Cleveland Indians (right) is named outstanding athlete of 1953.

George Mikan of the Minneapolis Lakers receives the award for greatest basketball player.

Joe Louis is named greatest prizefighter of the past 50 years.

Jesse Owens, star of the 1936 Olympics, is named greatest track star.

How many of these champions of the last century can you name?

WHAT A YEAR IT WAS!

golf

MASTERS	Sam Snead (3rd win)
U.S. AMATEUR	Arnold Palmer Barbara Romack
BRITISH OPEN	Peter Thomson
SENIOR PGA	Gene Sarazen

U.S. OPEN	Ed Furgol Babe Didrikson Zaharias
PGA	Chick Harbert
PGA/LPGA LEADING MONEY WINNER	Bob Toski $65,820 Patty Berg $16,011
PGA PLAYER OF THE YEAR	Ed Furgol

- A federal judge rules that Atlanta must allow blacks to use its public golf courses but may do so on a segregated basis.

- Under a temporary court order, pending completion of special golf courses for blacks, Nashville designates a public links for use by blacks two days a week.

- **Patty Berg** of Chicago tops the women's pro division for the second straight year for $5,000.

- **Frank Stranahan** of Toledo, Ohio wins his fifth straight world amateur title.

- **Arnold Palmer** turns professional this year.

TENNIS

U.S. OPEN

VIC SEIXAS over **REX HARTWIG**

DORIS HART over **LOUISE BROUGH**

WIMBLEDON

JAROSLAV DROBNY over **KEN ROSEWALL**

MAUREEN CONNOLLY over **LOUISE BROUGH**

DAVIS CUP

U.S. over AUSTRALIA, 3-2

The International Lawn Tennis Association rules in Paris to modify the foot-fault rule, a source of dispute between American and Australian Davis Cup teams, now making it permissible to swing one foot over the line during delivery.

1954

EZZARD CHARLES & ROCKY MARCIANO
IN TRAINING

Ezzard Charles (*far right*) hits the comeback trail, setting a stiff training pace in preparation for his June title bout with heavyweight champion **Rocky Marciano**.

Pointing to his more polished ring style and the aggressiveness he's shown in recent fights, his fans say it's a new Ezzard Charles going into the ring, not the fighter who was outpointed to lose the heavyweight crown, but a smooth, clever tiger who isn't fazed by the jinx that's defeated every ex-champ's attempt to regain the title.

Time out from training for a little friendly game of cards.

The Brockton Bomber has history on his side in the ring, as well as the most powerful right hand in the annals of boxing.

Other fighters may be more nimble, but the champ's footwork gets him into position for that blockbuster.

Marciano has been up against classy boxers before and all it takes is that one punch.

Rocky is favored to emerge the winner and continue as champion.

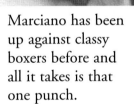

BOXING NEWS

A state appeals court in Austin, reversing a lower court decision in Dallas, rules that it is unconstitutional to bar boxing matches between black and white fighters.

19-year-old **Floyd Patterson** beats **Joe Gannon** in his first pro boxing victory.

☛ **HEAVYWEIGHT**
ROCKY MARCIANO

☛ **LIGHT HEAVYWEIGHT**
ARCHIE MOORE

☛ **MIDDLEWEIGHT**
CARL "BOBO" OLSON

☛ **WELTERWEIGHT**
KID GAVILAN
JOHNNY SAXTON

☛ **LIGHTWEIGHT**
JAMES CARTER
PADDY DEMARCO

☛ **FEATHERWEIGHT**
SANDY SADDLER

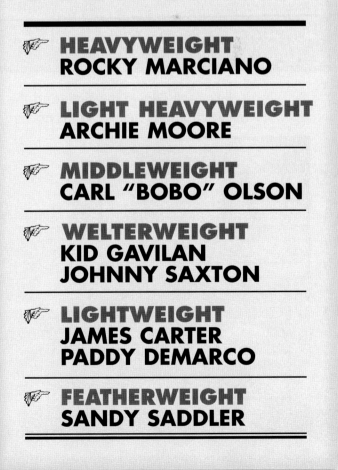

WHAT A YEAR IT WAS!

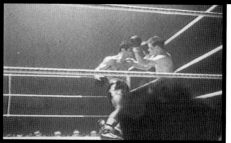

To this land of "Kellys" comes a "Cohen," a Frenchman seeking the European bantamweight crown.

Johnny Kelly holds the title, but down goes the pride of Ireland.

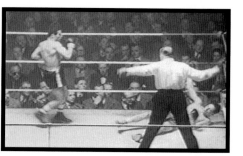

Kelly goes down again.

Kelly still has some fight left and he's up again.

Kelly's really down this time and the fallen champ is helped to his corner.

So **Bobby Cohen** is the champ and he's happy enough to cry.

Fans are suited up for this exciting match.

WHAT A YEAR IT WAS!

HORSE RACING

KENTUCKY DERBY
Determine, *ridden by* **Raymond York**

PREAKNESS STAKES
Hasty Road, *ridden by* **Johnny Adams**

BELMONT STAKES
High Gun, *ridden by* **Eric Guerin**

HORSE OF THE YEAR
Native Dancer

MONEY LEADERS
Jockey **Willie Shoemaker** $1,876,760

Horse **Determine** $328,700

Racing history is made at Agua Caliente, Mexico when **Mrs. Ottillia V. Alexander** of San Diego, California collects $12,274.80, the biggest daily double payoff in racing history.

•

Gordon Richards becomes first professional jockey to be knighted.

Figure Skating

U.S. Champions
- Hayes Jenkins
- Tenley Albright

World Champions
- Hayes Jenkins U.S.
- Gundi Busch West Germany

1954

SOCCER

WORLD CUP

West Germany over Hungary, 3-2

RODEO

ALL-AROUND
CHAMPION
COWBOY

BUCK RUTHERFORD

The *RACE* Is On

35,000 sports fans jam Empire Stadium in Vancouver for the **Mile of the Century.**

There's the gun and the start of the race. Six runners are competing, but the eyes of the world are on the two men who have completed the distance in less than four minutes—**Roger Bannister** of Harrow on the Hill, England, who performed the feat first, and **John Landy** of Australia, who shattered Bannister's record a month later in an international meet in Turku, Finland, completing the course in a record 3 minutes, 58 seconds.

Landy is in the lead with Bannister trailing on the final lap. The Australian took an early lead, setting a blistering pace the entire time, and now victory seems in his grasp.

But on the final turn Bannister passes him and drives hard for the tape.

A 25-year-old medical student at St. Mary's Hospital in London, Bannister wins and collapses into the arms of waiting friends.

What a finish! History has been made with the first double running of a mile in less than four minutes. Bannister's time: 3:58.8, Landy's time: 3:59.6.

TRACK & FIELD

BOSTON MARATHON
Veikko Karvonen, Finland

Wes Santee, America
4 min., 1.3 sec.
2nd fastest mile ever run to date

Diane Leather, England
4 min., 59.6 sec.
Fastest recorded women's mile

AAU DECATHLON TITLE
Rev. Bob Richards
America
15 ft.—world decathlon pole vault record

JAVELIN THROW
Nadezhda Konyayeva
Russia
180 ft., 8 in.

HIGH JUMP
Aleksandra Chudina
Russia
5 ft., 7 5/6 in.

1954

CYCLING

TOUR de FRANCE

Louison Bobet
France

SWIMMING

AAU SWIMMING MEET
Ford Konno, U.S.
(Triple Crown)

16-year-old **MARILYN BELL** *of Toronto becomes first person to swim 32 miles across Lake Ontario from Youngstown, NY to Sunnyside Beach, Ontario in 20 hrs., 56 min.*

CHESS

WORLD CHAMPIONS
Mikhail Botvinnik (U.S.S.R.)
Elizaveta Bykova (U.S.S.R.)

U.S. CHAMPIONS
Arthur Bisguier

Gisela K. Gresser wins U.S. Women's Open.

Russia defeats the U.S. 20-12 in a 32-game chess tournament held in New York.

CAR RACING

INDIANAPOLIS 500
Bill Vukovich
Fuel Injection Special,
130.84 mph

LE MANS
Froilan Gonzalez & Maurice Trintignant
Ferrari 375, 105.16 mph

WINSTON CUP
Lee Petty

Passings

Hugh Duffy, 87
Baseball Hall of Famer Duffy set a batting record of .438 in 1894 that remains unbroken today. He played for the Boston Nationals and later became a coach, manager and scout for different teams.

Glenn "Pop" Warner, 83
Lawyer-turned-football coach Warner achieved his greatest success as coach of Stanford University's team. In his long career, which included creating new maneuvers on the football field, he also coached at Iowa State, University of Georgia, Cornell University, Carlisle School for Indians, University of Pittsburgh and Temple University.

WHAT A YEAR IT WAS!

BILLIARDS

WORLD POCKET BILLIARD CHAMPION

Willie Mosconi

Mosconi runs a record 526 balls during an exhibition in Springfield, Ohio.

SOFTBALL

Men
Clearwater Bombers, Clearwater, FL

Women
Leach Motor Rockets, Fresno, CA

MAJOR FAST PITCH

DOG SHOW WINNER

WESTMINSTER KENNEL CLUB

Best in Show

Carmor's Rise and Shine

Cocker Spaniel

BOWLING

BPAA ALL-STAR TOURNAMENT — **DON CARTER MARION LADEWIG**

BOWLER OF THE YEAR — **DON CARTER MARION LADEWIG**
(5th year in a row)

Famous Births

Tony **Dorsett**
Chris **Evert**
Vince **Ferragamo**
Vitas **Gerulaitis**
Walter **Payton**
Ozzie **Smith**

ASSORTED AWARDS

1

AP ATHLETE OF THE YEAR
Willie Mays (Baseball)
Babe Didrikson Zaharias (Golf)

SPORTS ILLUSTRATED SPORTSMAN OF THE YEAR
Roger Bannister
track

JAMES E. SULLIVAN MEMORIAL AWARD
Mal Whitfield (Track)

THE HICKOK BELT
Willie Mays (Baseball)

WHAT A YEAR IT WAS!

1954 WAS A GREAT YEAR, BUT...

THE BEST IS YET TO COME!